Freedom, Inquiry,
and
Language

Freedom, Inquiry, and Language

W. EUGENE HEDLEY

University of California, Santa Barbara

INTERNATIONAL TEXTBOOK COMPANY

Scranton, Pennsylvania

The International Series in

Foundations of Education

Consulting Editor

HERBERT M. KLIEBARD

University of Wisconsin

To My Mother

Foreword

The unusual strength of *Freedom, Inquiry, and Language* can be appreciated only by comparing this book to recent work in philosophy of education. During the last few years publishing in this field has been very active. I have just counted on my study shelf thirty books that have been put out since 1964. This, of course, is far from a complete list. Despite the variety of points of view represented among these recent publications, all have a number of common tendencies. These are so marked that I am inclined to think a trend exists in current philosophy of education books. First, they are written much better than the average work on education. Second, they are intended for an audience of upper division or graduate students who have had no previous work in philosophy. Third, they are going deeper into the history of philosophy than previous work in this field. And last, in the latter chapters there is a nod in the direction of. "the new ideas" (existentialism and analytical philosophy). There are two more prominent tendencies: these books treat philosophical positions (pragmatism, existentialism, etc.) broadly and quite accurately *but not in depth;* furthermore, when principles developed by philosophers are applied to education, the results are vague and so broad as to be almost meaningless.

Turning now to Eugene Hedley's *Freedom, Inquiry, and Language,* several assumptions, questions, and answers are found in this book that set it apart from the current writing on the subject. Mr. Hedley makes the assumption that philosophical positions can be considered from the roots up only by penetrating the thinking of the men who have developed them, and not by relating generalizations about the high points of the school of thought as it has grown historically. He further assumes that acquaintance with philosophers of the ancient and medieval periods, as valuable as this may be for background, cannot and will not give the intellectual equipment required to see into today's thought. Such understanding comes only through long and rigorous study of contemporaries. Why such a demanding task seems particularly pertinent is clear when contemporary thinkers are read carefully, for they are revolutionary, building their concepts by the process of rejecting instated philosophical schools. A philosophical scholar may know his way around medieval or ancient thought, yet be completely baffled by twentieth century philosophy. Such bafflement clearly shows the scholar is ignorant of the world in which he lives. Furthermore, for all his knowledge of ancient thought, he has parted company with philosophy. For philosophy is not the study of how thinkers mastered problems of the past but of that emerging, developing, ordered conceptualization which is suited to dealing with today's world.

With these assumptions in mind, Mr. Hedley selects not pragmatism, existentialism, or analytical philosophy to focus his attention upon, but John Dewey, Jean-Paul Sartre, and Ludwig Wittgenstein. He does not then attempt a survey of these technically formidable philosophers, the usual approach in textbooks, but raises the question, ''What is the most characteristic and powerful concept each has developed?'' In responding to this question, Hedley selects and analyzes with unusual clarity and detail Dewey's *Theory of Inquiry,* Sartre's *Concept of Freedom,* and Wittgenstein's *Language Games.* Instead of pointing out what relevance these central ideas have for education in general, inquiry, freedom, and language analysis are sharply centered upon curriculum theory. There are few places in the literature of philosophy of education where a more tightly drawn relationship between philosophy and education can be found. This, of course, will be of value to the experienced reader. The exposition is so lucid, however, that a student just becoming acquainted with philosophy of education will have no difficulty understanding both the primary ideas of Dewey, Sartre, and Wittgenstein and how they can be related in an accurate way to twentieth century curriculum theory.

One of the continuing complaints heard over the years among those who make philosophy of education their profession is the dearth in philosophical studies that have something significant to say about education. What has been needed is a pattern or a model that will show how such a practical and moral undertaking as education can be enlightened by philosophical theory. Surely one form such a model will take will be found in Professor Eugene Hedley's *Freedom, Inquiry, and Language.*

Clyde E. Curran
The Claremont Graduate School
Claremont, California

Preface

The present work was undertaken with several purposes in mind. First, although the entire history of philosophy contains a vast array of insights of potential value for the educator, it is contemporary philosophy that focuses upon areas of most immediate concern to society in general and to the educator in particular. Second, the limited time allowed for students who are preparing to become teachers to spend in exploring the social and philosophical foundations of education requires that this small amount of time be concentrated upon issues of most immediate concern. Third, it is hoped that this work will provide an example of at least one way of relating philosophy to education, rather than providing *a* philosophy of education. Fourth, this work is intended to serve as either a basic text in a course in the philosophy of education or as a supplementary text in the more general "social foundations" type of course. Finally, because of the emphasis placed upon relating the three philosophic concepts to curriculum theory, this work should prove of interest to those concerned with the more basic and initial steps in the construction of curriculum theory.

W. EUGENE HEDLEY

Santa Barbara, California
March, 1968

ix

Contents

xi

chapter 1

Introduction

There is much bemoaning the ills of contemporary society. Such laments, of course, are not an uncommon entry in the history of mankind. What seems to add concern to the rising modern chorus of laments is the growing awareness that some of these contemporary ailments might well prove to be fatal. This awareness stems in part from the increasing feeling of impotency experienced by individuals in our modern society. Particularly, individuals feel powerless to control or even influence the development of the rapidly expanding technologies and the institutions that employ and/or develop these technologies. Not only "push-button" wars and "push-button" defenses leave the individual with feelings of impotency, but the political institutions that supposedly do exert control over the "buttons" are felt by the individual to be too remote from his sphere of influence for him to have any effect on the institutional decisions.

Among the diagnosticians concerned with the ailments of modern society there seems to be little agreement as to the precise nature of the ills; a lack of consensus as to possible solutions naturally follows. However, one general description of the contemporary scene seems to be commonly held: modern society suffers from a steady proliferation of means with an accompanying confusion of ends. The ends are seen in this case to be those values which will allow the individual to evaluate the decisions of institutions and the uses to which the technologies will be put. Nevertheless, an agreement on such a generalized proposition fails to provide much guidance toward a cure, for what are the ends or goals or values of our society?

To ask for the ends, goals, or values of a society seems at best a "meaningless" question. Still, if it is acknowledged at the onset that the notion of "society" is an abstraction and thus cannot directly give an answer, and further that what a society by way of a consensus allows to be said of itself is not always a true representation of its goals and values, then certain pitfalls may be avoided and the question becomes more meaningful. The question has significance only if it is agreed that the appropriate criterion for determining the values of a society rests in the various activities in which the individual members of the society engage themselves—not in what they say about the activities, but in what they actually do.

The task of extracting the *values* of a society from the *activities* of its members is not novel. While it has only been in most recent times that a scientific effort has been made in this direction (an effort required to provide the precision necessary for the formulation of some prescriptions capable of full implementation), philosophers for over twenty-five hundred years have reflected in their inquiries the concerns and the values of their societies. The concern over the decline of Athenian society during the last part of the fifth century B.C. was reflected in the moral, social, and political emphasis found in the Platonic dialogues. The seventeenth century concern over the issue of authority and freedom found expression in the works of Thomas Hobbes and others. There is little need to further elaborate this point; let it suffice to say that there is at least one other place to which a person can go other than to the behavior of large numbers of individuals in order to gain some clarification of the ends, goals, and values of a society, and that place is to the philosophers. These men, in their activities as philosophers, do reflect to some extent the values of their times. A philosopher is no more able than any other human being to operate in a vacuum; his interest is also the interest of the age in which he lives and works. In addition, the very nature of the philosophic activity requires that the philosopher take into account the widest possible spectrum of activities that comprise the human enterprise of his times. Thus, the success of a philosopher is related to that philosopher's sensitivity to the values, ends, and goals implicit in the overall pattern of activities engaged in by the members of his society.

At least for purposes of this work, it will be assumed that the analyses presented by modern philosophers will reveal the concerns and values of our contemporary society. Some of these concerns and values are, of course, perennial. However, if it it is desirable to gain some insight into the direction in which contemporary society is moving, then most likely it will be ascertained by looking into those philosophies which constitute in some measure a departure from the traditional concerns and methods of philosophy.

It must now be asked: What contemporary philosophies constitute a departure from the perennial concerns and/or methods, and how are they related to the concerns of modern society? The three areas of modern philosophic concern that would seem to depart most from the perennial concerns are existentialism, pragmatism, and language analysis.

Existential philosophers express the concern of Western society with the freedom and integrity of the individual in the face of feelings of impotency resulting from the increased bureaucratization of society and its institutions. These philosophers have revived and reinstituted the dialectic method in order to present the human situation in a perspective that allows the individual to surmount his feelings of alienation from and impotency in a mass society. The dialectic method is, of course, as old as Plato and it has a long heritage in Western thought. What is novel and of interest is the existentialists' application of this method concurrently with developments in the field of psychology stemming from the revived humanistic concerns engendered by the mass culture of the West and its "threats" to individual dignity and freedom.

Pragmatism evidences in its works a primary concern with problem solving. The particular orientation of pragmatism is toward the methodology of problem solving. Using physical science as a model, pragmatism has sought to describe the characteristic method of the physical sciences in such a manner as to account for the apparent success of physical science in resolving its "problems." Pragmatism further expresses a major concern with the increasing number of social problems and the noticeable lack of success in resolving them. Involved in this concern is the pressing problem of the relation of the individual to society. Pragmatism seeks to demonstrate the relevance of the method of modern science to the solution of social problems. Thus, too, does pragmatism reflect man's concern with attaining greater understanding and, hence, control over his social environment—a concern exemplified not only in philosophy but in the modern development of the social "sciences."

Ordinary language analysis—referring to those philosophers who follow the kind of concern evidenced by the later work of Ludwig Wittgenstein—represents a philosophic activity which seeks to reveal the source and function of ordinary language. While such philosophic activity focuses upon the perplexities arising within philosophy itself, this activity bears directly upon the problems that arise from the increasing demands upon language in dealing with the complexities of modern society and the increasing dependency of society upon symbolic forms. The need to increasingly refine the distinctions among the various functions of language has never been more pressing. Or perhaps, the need still exists just to recognize that ordinary language has more than one function—a matter that escaped the attention of earlier philosophers.

What has been previously asserted about contemporary society was meant to be applied quite directly to that social institution which as much as, if not more than, any other reflects the present state of society, namely, the school. It is certainly true that the present state of education reflects the proliferation of means and the confusion of ends which surely characterizes our age. Consider what is "new" on the educational scene! The "new math" clearly offers no novelty to the field of mathematics itself. What is new is the manner of presenting the content of mathematics to would-be learners. The value of mathematics itself is not questioned. The same is true of the Physical Science Study Committee's course in physics, as well as the courses in biology, structural linguistics, and so forth. Other means that currently threaten to escalate the proliferation are the educational use of such innovations as simulations and television. All these means fail to contribute to any clarification of educational goals or values. It may be said that these newly developed and developing means rest upon a basic assumption: the maintence of the *status quo* insofar as the basic structure and content of the curriculum are concerned. For example, few if any of the individuals involved in producing the new means ever seriously consider a question such as "Why teach physics in the high school?" Why, indeed, physics? What is it that physics, for example, can do for all or most of our youth that makes it indispensable to their education and that cannot be done better by some other study or activity? How is it possible to evaluate any means without first having some clear idea of some end-in-view?

The following chapters will be principally concerned with the educational implication of the views of three philosophers whose works exert a major influence in the contemporary philosophical scene. More specifically, the following chapters will draw one of the more important concepts from each of the philosophers chosen, and, after a complete description, each concept will be examined as a possible goal or basis for the development of a curriculum theory.

It is not within the scope of this work to enter into a discussion concerning the nature of curriculum theory or the nature of theory itself. For the present purpose it will suffice to consider "theory" in its broadest meaning. In some instances "theory" will designate assertions of basic assumptions and values. In other instances "theory" will refer to prescriptive judgments concerning procedures. Finally, "theory" may also include statements concerning general organizing principles. In all cases the meaning of "theory" is intended to include *at least* these three components; the exclusion of one or more is merely an indication that the particular philosophic concept under consideration is not relevant to the entire range of meaning usually covered by the term "theory."

Part One of this work will consider the philosophic views of Jean-Paul Sartre and their implications for education and curriculum theory. That Jean-Paul Sartre is the key figure in the development of modern existential thought seems incontestable; that his particular view remains unrelated to educational philosophy seems incomprehensible. In Part One, Sartre's central concept of "absolute freedom" will be fully described and them employed as a basis for the development of a curriculum theory.

Part Two of the present work deals with the philosophy of John Dewey, which has often been related to the philosophy of education and to educational practices, not only by contemporary educators but by Dewey himself. It seems strange, in light of the numerous writings which apply Dewey's philosophy to the educational scene, that so central a concept as Dewey's theory of inquiry should have escaped with but slight attention. Thus, we will seek in some small way to remedy the situation. Dewey's theory of inquiry will be fully expounded with a distinction drawn between scientific and social inquiry. The theory of inquiry will then be set forth as the basis for the development of a curriculum theory. Where available, Dewey's own recommendations will be followed. It is intended that such a process will illuminate the implications for curriculum theory of this most fundamental concept.

Part Three will be concerned with the later philosophy of Ludwig Wittgenstein whose work, *Philosophical Investigations*,[1] has proved an important milestone in the development of ordinary language analysis. From this vital work Wittgenstein's analogy of "language games" will be selected as representing in a most concise form the view of language developed in *Philosophical Investigations*. After describing how this analogy reflects Wittgenstein's view of language, the analogy will be applied to several terms important to dealing with both language and education. The analogy of language games is then examined as a basis for a curriculum theory; in so doing, the implications of Wittgenstein's view of language for education and curriculum theory are made explicit. That such an undertaking is desirable is clear when it is noted that such an outstanding contribution to contemporary philosophy remains as yet unrelated to the area of educational philosophy in a specific manner.

The concluding chapter of this work will pose the question of whether or not the curriculum and educational implications developed from these three contemporary philosophic positions share any elements in common. In short, do these three philosophers have any common concerns that bear directly upon either curriculum theory or education in general?

Finally, it should be noted that this work is meant to be exploratory rather than prescriptive. Three philosophical concepts are being ex-

---

[1] Ludwig Wittgenstein, *Philosophical Investigations*, translated by G. E. M. Anscombe (New York: The Macmillan Co., 1953).

plored for possible implications for the development of curriculum theory particularly, and for education in general. In other words, to what extent do the concerns of these philosophers reflect or relate to the concerns of education? To what extent do these philosophies suggest meaningful goals or values for the direction of the "means" at the disposal of the educator? There is no intention here to recommend or prescribe one or more of these resulting "theories" for adoption or practical implementation. Rather, the purpose is to make the implications clear so that others may determine whether or not the research prerequisite to any application would be warranted. Some of the more obvious "prerequisite" considerations will be mentioned in the course of this book.

part One

Freedom and Education

chapter 2

The Analysis of Absolute Freedom

INTRODUCTION

During the past two decades existentialism has passed from philosophy to fad and back again to philosophy. Seldom has a philosophy received such wide notoriety, not all of which was justified or philosophically relevant. What then is this philosophy of existence? What makes it warrant special attention? In contrast to most modern philosophies, existentialism chooses as its starting point the everyday, concrete experiences of mankind, rather than the problems of language or epistemology. Existentialism seeks to discover the means by which man can create his own meaning out of the situation in which he finds himself. The nature of the human situation then becomes an area of concern for the existentialist. Human existence is the basic fact with which existentialists build their philosophy. The essence of man is created by man himself. It is this basic appeal of existentialism to the fundamental human condition that accounts for its popular appeal as well as its significant contribution to philosophy itself.

> The existential philosophers themselves have taught us to reread in a new and more profound way the whole history of modern thought. By showing us philosophy as an essentially human enterprise they have enabled us to see the whole history of philosophy for the momentous human drama it really is.[1]

Jean-Paul Sartre is undoubtedly the most widely known of the existential philosophers. He is also the most widely discussed existentialist, both as a person and as a novelist as well as philosopher. Jean-Paul Sartre is one of the few philosophers that are most often labeled "existentialists" who does not seek to avoid the title and even willingly makes use of it. Sartre certainly stands as a key figure in the contemporary development of existentialism.

[1] William Barrett and H. D. Aiken, eds., *Philosophy in the Twentieth Century* (New York: Random House, 1962), Vol. 111, p. 144.

To understand Jean-Paul Sartre is to understand something important about the present time. As philosopher, as politician, and as novelist Sartre is profoundly and self-consciously contemporary; he has the style of the age. The landscape of his activity exhibits to us the development of this style as a natural growth out of the European tradition of thought on ethics, metaphysics and politics. Connections which elsewhere are subterranean stand clearly traced out in the prolific lucidity of Sartre's work.[2]

As a philosopher, Sartre is squarely in the European tradition. His debts to Hegel, Kierkegaard, and Husserl are clear. His dependence upon the Cartesian "cogito" is clearly discernible. His starting point, as William Barrett points out, is analogous to that of Descartes, but with one monumental difference. Through his systematic doubt, Descartes brought himself to the basic truth, *"Cogito ergo sum."* However, he rescued himself from the realm of utter subjectivity by a questionable bit of reasoning that affirmed the existence of God and, consequently, a system of transcendent absolute values. Sartre, on the other hand, is a Descartes in the twentieth century. He has behind him the violent eruptions of the nineteenth century, epitomized in Nietzsche's proclamation of the death of God. Like Descartes, Sartre has penetrated to the essential truth, "I think, I reflect, therefore I exist." But for Sartre there can be no syllogistic recourse to God and transcendental truth. Man can be certain only of his existence, an existence that he awakens to without having chosen it; he can be certain only of his thoughts and actions in a world that he did not make and that is largely unintelligible to him.

> Sartre is a Cartesian who has read Proust and Heidegger, and whose psychological explorations of man go far beyond those of the seventeenth-century philosopher; more important still, he is a Cartesian who has experienced war and terror in the modern world and who is therefore situated historically in an altogether different relation to the world. But a Cartesian he is, nonetheless, as perhaps no Frenchman—or no French thinker—can help being when the chips are really down. Descartes and the French Resistance—these are the simple keys to the whole of Sartre's apparently complicated and involved philosophy.[3]

Thus, Sartre is a philosopher in the finest European tradition, and certainly he is not the eccentric or sensationalist that many journalists would make him.

Before beginning a detailed discussion of Sartre's analysis of freedom, a brief overview of Sartre's philosophy of existence will help to locate "freedom" and indicate its central position in the existentialism of

---

[2] Iris Murdoch, *Sartre: Romantic Rationalist* (New Haven: Yale University Press, 1953), p. vii.

[3] William Barrett, *Irrational Man* (New York: Doubleday and Company, 1958), p. 242.

Sartre. However, only in the more extensive discussion of freedom itself can a true picture of this philosophy be given.

Sartre begins his philosophy at the only certain starting point: man's subjectivity. All man's knowledge must begin with his own awareness of himself as an undefined, conscious existent with the capacity and need to sustain and fulfill himself through interaction with his environment. He comprehends and designs himself only through his projects.

> For we mean that man first exists, that is, that man first of all is the being who hurls himself toward a future and who is conscious of imagining himself as being in the future. Man is at the start a plan which is aware of itself, . . .[4]

Man is thus aware first of his existence; then, through his projects, he constructs his essence.

The existentialism of Jean-Paul Sartre places the responsibility for man's existence squarely upon his own shoulders. Man makes himself through his own choices. But in making his choices a man also projects and creates an image of all mankind. A man may choose for himself, but in the process he chooses for all men. To accept what has now become the slogan of existentialism, "existence precedes essence," is to reject any *a priori* standard of human nature. Therefore, there is nothing determining a man's choice. Man is free, man is his freedom, for it is man who creates human nature. Sartre goes even further and asserts that man is condemned to be free.[5] He is "condemned" in the same sense that a man does not create his existence, but from the first instant of his existence he is and becomes all that mankind is and becomes.

If man's choices are not determined by some *a priori* view of human nature, then surely such choices find limitation in the human situation. What choice is there concerning the time or place of man's existence? Who can choose to walk through a mountain rather than over it? Certainly such limitations are there; they are always encountered and recognized. However, man does not exist apart from the human situation but in relation to it. And it is for a man to freely determine the particular relation these factors of the human situation will have to him. It is by choosing these relationships that a man determines himself and his existence. A mountain is a source of pleasure to the mountain climber and an obstacle to the highway engineer. Freedom is nihilation. Freedom is absolute. Understanding the full meaning of these propositions requires more than the cursory treatment given above. The preceding paragraphs have sufficed to indicate that freedom is a central thesis of Sartre's

---

[4] Jean-Paul Sartre, *Existentialism and Human Emotions* (New York: Philosophical Library, 1957), p. 16.
[5] *Ibid.*, p. 23.

philosophy. Also, no adequate description of Sartre's philosophy can avoid the concept of freedom, or can any description of Sartre's notion of freedom fail to reveal the essential portion of Sartre's philosophy.

In the remainder of this chapter Sartre's analysis of freedom will be described in some detail. The sense in which freedom is absolute will also be discussed. And finally, applications of absolute freedom to the topics of knowledge and ethics will be presented.

THE ANALYSIS OF FREEDOM

Sartre unfolds or reveals his concept of freedom in a number of ways, both in abstract and in concrete situations. His abstract development is encountered most generally in philosophical treatises, while Sartre's plays and novels present freedom in and through concrete situations. For the purposes of this study, "freedom" will be revealed in the consideration of five assertions concerning the nature of human existence, and will follow in general the development presented in Part Four of Sartre's major philosophical work *Being and Nothingness*.[6] The five assertions are as follows. (1) To exist is to act; that is to say, an individual's existence is inseparable from the totality of his acts. (2) The fundamental condition of an act is freedom. (3) Freedom arises in an act of nihilation of "being-in-itself" by "being-for-itself." (4) Freedom is identical with or at least indistinguishable from being-for-itself (human consciousness). (5) Freedom manifests itself to consciousness in the feeling of anguish. Each of these five assertions will now be developed in turn.

Consciousness appears in the world. This is the starting of existential ontology, the "given," the basic assumption. For without consciousness there is no human existence. Consciousness appears in the world without reason, without purpose; it is "thrown in." The awareness of consciousness as such occurs only by abstraction, for consciousness does not reveal itself except as consciousness of something. Consciousness appears in the world but it is not a part of the world. The world comprises everything that is; therefore, consciousness, which is other than the world, is nothing or "nothingness." By what process does consciousness relate to the world? The world of things or being-in-itself exists simply as an undifferentiated "given." Consciousness, which is "nothingness," accomplishes the differentiation of the "given" through acts of nihilation. Consciousness may act upon everything that "is," that is, nihilation being-in-itself. "To act upon" implies "being outside of"; hence, that

---

[6] Jean-Paul Sartre, *Being and Nothingness,* translated by Hazel E. Barnes (New York: Philosophical Library, 1956).

which is outside of everything must be other than things or no things; nothingness. Thus, conscious existence or human existence cannot be separated from the act of nihilation. The meaning of existence is inseparable from those acts which are consciousness. Thus, human reality does not exist first in order to act later; but for human reality, "to be is to act, and to cease to act is to cease to be."[7]

The fundamental condition of the act is freedom. The full meaning of this statement lies in the relation between consciousness and action. Sartre rejects as inadequate the common notions of "cause" and "motive" as explanations of actions. Actions are said to be "caused" by some concrete situation or "motivated" by some state of mind. However, the concrete situation "is"; the state of mind "is." How can that which "is" motivate or cause that which "is not"? "But if human reality is action, this means evidently that its determination to action is itself action."[8] In short, it is the action of consciousness that initially determines the content of any concrete situation and differentiates it from the "given." Therefore, a person selects that state of affairs which is later said to "cause his act." The same is true of states of mind. The way a person chooses to relate himself to being-in-itself will provide the "state of mind."

For example, it might be asserted that the Sixteenth Amendment to the United States Constitution "causes" me to pay income tax. Sartre would refuse this assertion. What causes the paying of income tax is the selection by an individual of a state of affairs in which paying taxes is an attendant part. A state of affairs, such as a prison term, could equally well have been selected and paying taxes would not have been an attendant part, or another country might have been selected, or a life with no income, and many others. Another example might be the case of a thief who claims that he cannot help but steal because of early experiences with poverty. Again, Sartre would reject such a claim. The thief has chosen to relate himself to an impoverished situation in an antisocial way. Others in similar situations have made other choices.

What then "causes" consciousness to differentiate in one way rather than another? An act "must be defined by an intention."[9] The intention comes into being in the act of choosing ends which in turn make the intention known. Hence, the fundamental condition of the act would seem to be "freedom," freedom in the sense that ends are only "determined" by what is not, and an individual's intention is revealed only in his choice of ends, not by a factual state of affairs or mind.

[7] *Ibid.*, p. 476.
[8] *Ibid.*
[9] *Ibid.*, p. 477.

Freedom arises in the action of the nihilation of being-in-itself by being-for-itself. Because consciousness (or being-for-itself) is essentially "nothingness" it is not involved in a causal relationship with the world of being-in-itself. Consciousness is thereby free, free from causal contingency. Consciousness brings nothingness into the world so that it can nihilate.

> To nihilate means to be dissatisfied with the raw existent and to transform it into something that will conform more closely to my intentions.[10]

Consciousness is grounded in the world but it not determined by it. Being-for-itself is conscious of itself as existent, but it requires no other existent or is it determined by other existents. Therefore, consciousness is free and without foundation.

> This characteristic of the for-itself implies that it is the being which finds *no help, no pillar of support* in what it *was*.[11]

Human consciousness is not only free, it is indistinguishable from freedom itself.

> Therefore the freedom of the for-itself appears as its *being*. But since this freedom is neither a given nor a property, it can be only by choosing itself. The freedom of the for-itself is always *engaged;* there is no question here of a freedom which could be undetermined and which would pre-exist its choice. We shall never apprehend ourselves except as a choice in the making. But freedom is simply the fact that this choice is always unconditioned.[12]

Finally, the manifestation of freedom to consciousness in the feeling of anguish must be explained. Freedom arises out of the act of free choice which is inevitable, inescapable. Choices like consciousness itself may be "unconditioned" and without foundation, but a person cannot not choose. Even a decision not to choose involves a choice. It is in the feeling of anguish that an individual becomes aware of the facts concerning his freedom: the fact that he must choose; the fact that his choices are unconditioned; the fact that his freedom is without foundation; the fact that he seeks to exist as part of the world, but is forever "condemned to be free" and forever "condemned" to becoming through his choices.

> The anguish which, when this possibility is revealed, manifests our freedom to our consciousness is witness of this perpetual modifiability of our initial project. In anguish we do not simply apprehend the fact

---

[10] Justice Streller, *Jean-Paul Sartre: To Freedom Condemned,* translated by Wade Baskin (New York: Philosophical Library, 1960), p. 139.

[11] Sartre, *Being and Nothingness,* p. 479.

[12] *Ibid.*

that the possibles which we project are perpetually eaten away by our freedom-to-come; in addition we apprehend our choice—i.e., ourselves as *unjustifiable*.[13]

Next, it should be noted that freedom arises as freedom only because there is the "brute-in-itself" in which projects are realized. It is only by acting upon a world of things (and in a world of things) that human freedom is revealed.

> The technical and philosophical concept of freedom, the only one which we are considering here, means only the autonomy of choice. It is necessary, however, to note that the choice, being identical with acting, supposes a commencement of realization in order that the choice may be distinguished from the dream and the wish.[14]

This "commencement" occurs as part of the in-itself, and there arises here a paradox. It would seem that freedom exists only in concrete situations and that the concrete situation can exist only by virtue of an individual's freedom. If this paradoxical aspect of human reality were accepted without further analysis, then the individual's freedom would indeed be absolute. However, closer examination reveals that freedom encounters resistances and obstacles that have not been created by freedom. If Sartre's concept of freedom is to retain any meaning, he must show how such ready-made situations do not limit individual freedom. There are certain factors within situations which seem to be "predetermined" and hence impose limits upon freedom. Sartre selects five such "structures of the situation" for examination: the individual's place, his past, his environment, his fellow men, and his death. Each of these will be considered briefly.

First, a person's facticity, his being-in-the-world, is in some sense determined by his place. By his "place" Sartre means his geographical location, which would include country, climate, and so forth. However, "the facticity of my place is revealed to me only in and through the free choice which I make of my end."[15] In other words, whether or not a person's place constitutes an obstacle or aid to his freely chosen end is determined by the end itself. Also, the freedom to transform (nihilate) his place in accord with some end presupposes and initially "given" place. The individual's place then as a part of the structure of his situation appears as a necessary condition of his freedom.

For a person to find himself placed in the northern polar regions will not itself have any meaning. Such a place takes on meaning only when the individual begins to posit projects or ends for himself. If an Eskimo

---

[13] *Ibid.*, p. 464.
[14] *Ibid.*, p. 483.
[15] *Ibid.*, p. 494.

chooses to become a great hunter of seals or herder of caribou, then his place takes on a meaning as an assisting factor in realizing his project. On the other hand, if the same Eskimo chooses to become a great skin diver then his place takes on the meaning of a handicap to the achievement of such an end. The point is that the ''place'' must first exist before any meaning can be given to it. It is the Eskimo's free choice of ends that gives meaning to the ice and snow, and hence, his ''place'' is a requirement for his freedom. Without something to be transformed, choices are merely idealizations or dreams.

The same condition prevails with respect to the past. A person's past must be ''irremediable'' in order that he may have a basis from which to change. On the other hand, the past derives its meaning solely from an individual's present project. This does not mean that his past acts can have just any meaning, but that his present project will determine the bearing these acts will have in obstructing or promoting his present project.

> Who shall decide whether that mystic crisis in my fifteenth year ''was'' a mere accident of puberty or, on the contrary, the first sign of a future conversion? I myself, according to whether I shall decide—at twenty years of age, at thirty years—to be converted. The project of conversion by a single stroke confers on an adolescent crisis the value of a premonition which I had not taken seriously. Who shall decide whether the period which I spent in prison after a theft was fruitful or deplorable? I—according to whether I give up stealing or become hardened. Who can decide the educational value of a trip, the sincerity of a profession of love, the purity of a past intention, etc.? It is I, always I, according to the ends by which I illuminate these past events.[16]

The third aspect of the structure of the human situation as considered by Sartre is that of the environment. By environment is meant those instrumental things which surround the individual including their utility value. Again, the meaning of the environment is determined only by a specific projected end.

> To be free is to-be-free-to-change. Freedom implies therefore the existence of an environment to be changed: obstacles to be cleared, tools to be used. Of course it is freedom which reveals them as obstacles, but by its free choice it can only interpret the *meaning* of their being.[17]

However, it is within the structure of the environment that the unpredictable enters into the situation. The introduction of a new instrument can radically change the situation itself. Nevertheless, this in no way changes the present project of an individual, but may change the

16 *Ibid.*, p. 498.
17 *Ibid.*, p. 506.

meaning of certain aspects of his environment from obstacles to aids or from aids to obstacles.

> Every free project in projecting itself anticipates a margin of unpredictability due to the independence of things precisely because this independence is that in terms of which freedom is constituted. As soon as I project going to the nearby village to find Pierre, the punctures, the "headwind," a thousand forseeable and unforseeable accidents are given in my project and constitute its meaning. Thus the unexpected puncture which upsets my projects comes *to take its place* in a world pre-outlined by my choice, for I have never ceased, if I may say so, to *expect it as unexpected.*[18]

The fourth element of human facticity is one's fellow man. An individual finds himself engaged in a world in which instruments and his place possess meanings not of his own choosing but supplied by others. Such ready-made meanings may condition a person's freedom but they do not limit it. The existence of others, however, does limit the individual's freedom. For when another consciousness or freedom presents itself to an individual, the individual finds himself giving a meaning which he has neither chosen nor is able to appropriate. It is a meaning that can only be endured. Yet, this is the only condition under which a person can recognize the freedom of another.

> I see that there is a liberty beyond my liberty, a situation beyond my situation, and that this involves my being there in the middle of the world for someone else, and by willing that situation and reacting to it in the circumstances of my particular case I bring it into my situation under my liberty, although it remains unrealizable.[19]

To be an American is first and foremost a meaning or label attached to those born within the territorial limits of the United States. A person does not choose to be so classed but is given this label by others. The situation of "being an American" is unrealizable. This is to say, it is an abstraction—a meaning not created by the individual but by others. Try as he will, the individual can never fulfill the requirements that exist in other consciousnesses. The individual can, however, choose to accept the situation of "being an American" and thereby continue to freely posit individual ends within the situation of "being an American," but without being able to realize the end posited for him by others. Not to will this situation is to confront a limit to freedom, for a person cannot not be an American any more than a person cannot not be a Negro. Only by refusing to will the freedom of others will an individual's freedom encounter limits.

[18] *Ibid.,* p. 507

[19] H. J. Blackham, *Six Existentialist Thinkers* (New York: Harper Torch Books, Harper & Brothers, Inc., 1952), p. 135.

Death may be considered as another factor in the human situation, an element of facticity. Sartre insists that a person's death belongs to his facticity as a contingent fact. However, it can never become a part of his situation because it exists only as for-others and can never be encountered by the for-itself. Thus, it is only because a person's freedom never encounters his death that his death does not limit his freedom.

To summarize, the human situation is, then, the totality of an individual's being. That is to say, it is the total facticity, including the absolute contingency of the world, as illuminated by the nihilation of the in-itself by the for-itself and given meaning by freely posited projects or goals. The human situation is neither subjective nor objective. It is not subjective because impressions are not the source of the individual's situation; he finds himself in a world of things that simply *are there* and cannot be otherwise. The human situation is not objective because the meaning of "my situation" can only be supplied through the freedom of consciousness in the activity of positing ends. The human situation may also be said to be concrete, for human consciousness never aims at fundamentally abstract or universal ends. Consciousness is always involved in the process of revealing itself to itself. Also, the situation cannot be said to be the result of individual freedom, or can it be said to be a collection of obstacles to individual freedom. Rather, a person's situation may be viewed as the illumination of his facticity by his freedom, and in the process it determines what are to be obstacles.

> It is by the assumption of this contingency and by its surpassing that there can be at once a *choice* and an organization of things in *situation;* and it is the contingency of freedom and the contingency of the in-itself which are expressed *in situation* by the unpredictability and the adversity of the environment. Thus I am absolutely free and absolutely responsible for my situation. But I am never free except *in situation.*[20]

Before describing some applications of Sartre's "absolute freedom," a few words concerning the absoluteness of freedom will be appropriate. Freedom or human consciousness is absolute in the sense that

> . . . each person is an absolute choice of self from the standpoint of a world of knowledges and of techniques which this choice both assumes and illumines.[21]

To be conscious is to be conscious of something, and this "something" is determined only by consciousness itself in an act of free choice. This free choice is ultimately unjustified and unjustifiable—it is inescapable and absolute. Human freedom is also absolute in the sense of "unlimited."

[20] Sartre, *Being and Nothingness*, p. 509.
[21] Sartre, *Existentialism and Human Emotions*, p. 56.

The human situation cannot limit freedom, for it is the individual's choice that gives meaning to the situation and the situation always admits a possibility of choice. As Sartre says in his essay on "Cartesian Freedom," "To be free is not to be able to do what one wants but to want what one can."[22] So long as consciousness exists, there is nihilation, there is the "No!"

THE APPLICATION OF ABSOLUTE FREEDOM

The first application of Sartre's notion of absolute freedom will be to the area of knowledge. How is knowledge dealt with from the perspective of absolute freedom? "There is only intuitive knowledge,"[23] says Sartre. Formal processes of reasoning such as deduction are only means leading to intuition. Knowledge is, in a sense, the essence of consciousness:

> Knowledge appears then as a mode of being. Knowing is neither a relation established after the event between two beings, nor is it an activity of one of these two beings, nor is it a quality of a property or a virtue. It is the very being of the for-itself in so far as this is presence to—; that is, in so far as the for-itself has to be its being by making itself not to be a certain being to which it is present.[24]

Thus, knowledge is not describable as a relation, quality, or activity. Knowledge arises intuitively when consciousness gives itself up to an object to such an extent that all other objects in the world become nihilated and even consciousness itself is reduced to the slightest awareness of itself as distinct from the object. Sartre provides an excellent example of this immediate fact of knowing:

> A psychological and empirical exemplification of this original relation is furnished us in the case of *fascination*. In fascination, which represents the immediate fact of *knowing,* the knower is absolutely nothing but a pure negation; he does not find or recover himself anywhere—he *is not.* The only qualification which he can support is that he *is not* precisely this particular fascinating object. In fascination there is nothing more than a gigantic object in a desert world. Yet the fascinated intuition is in no way a *fusion* with the object. In fact the condition necessary for the existence of fascination is that the object be raised in absolute relief on a background of emptiness; that is, I am precisely the immediate negation of the object and nothing but that.[25]

---

[22] Jean-Paul Sartre, *Literary and Philosophical Essays,* translated by Annette Michelson (New York: Collier Books, 1962), p. 184.

[23] Sartre, *Being and Nothingness,* p. 172.

[24] *Ibid.,* p. 174.

[25] *Ibid.,* p. 177.

Human consciousness or freedom makes the world appear, and as it appears consciousness directly intuits, incorporates it within itself. "Knowledge is assimilation."[26] In this sense, knowing can be considered as a form of appropriation. For knowledge so obtained is "my knowledge." It is through an individual's freedom that a portion of the world is revealed. It is to that individual that the portion of the world reveals itself.

It is through acts of nihilation that specific knowledge comes into being. A person comes to know this house as he becomes conscious that at this particular moment it is "not that house" and "not that house." By relegating all the world except "this house" to nonexistence, "this house" appears and is intuitively appropriated or becomes known. All specific characteristics or attributes of knowledge such as quantity and potentiality are represented by Sartre as means by which human freedom organized the world or being-in-itself. They exist as part of the nihilation function of consciousness and not in the world. The only exception to this is quality, which for Sartre "is nothing other than the being of the *this* when it is considered apart from the external relation with the world or other *thises*."[27] Quality is the object revealing itself to consciousness as an existing thing; in itself quality adds nothing to being except its "thisness."

In terms of knowledge, Sartre's notion of absolute freedom leaves him in a position to be classed equally as a realist (which he claims) or as an idealist. As Wilfred Desan concludes:

> To be exact, one could consider Sartre both as a realist and as an idealist; as a realist because he accepts the "brute existent" as being independent of human intervention, and as an idealist because he charges human consciousness (or For-itself) with the task of giving meaning or significance to this "brute existent."[28]

FREEDOM AND ETHICS

Turning now to the matter of ethics, absolute freedom and its attendant absolute responsibility gives to all human endeavors a moral dimension:

> Reflective consciousness can be properly called a moral consciousness since it can not arise without at the same moment disclosing values.[29]

[26] *Ibid.*, p. 579.

[27] *Ibid.*, p. 186.

[28] Wilfred Desan, *The Tragic Finale* (Harper Torch Books, Harper & Brothers, Inc., 1954), p. 56.

[29] Sartre, *Being and Nothingness*, p. 95.

Sartre himself has not yet provided a detailed existential ethic; however, the moral tone attached to the authentic life is clearly revealed in his fictional works, particularly in his plays. To apply absolute freedom to human behavior is to prescribe a way of life. In the following pages some of the salient features of moral conduct based upon absolute freedom will be presented.

The first feature of existential ethics is derived from Sartre's position that absolute freedom is both unsupported and unsupportable. Because freedom is unsupported or ungrounded, there can be no *a priori* basis upon which to make a choice. This excludes the possibility of basing choices on an appeal to a prior psychological state or "the unconscious." The uncaused nature of absolute freedom also precludes any external stimuli from determining a choice; the individual's freedom gives meaning to any such stimuli. Because freedom is unsupportable, that is, not justifiable on any external or objective basis, there can be no appeal to either moral absolutes or social standards as a basis for a choice. Man is "condemned" to be free, and his acts which are the expression of his freedom are totally and absolutely his.

How, then, do values come into existence? Absolute freedom or the individual consciousness is the sole foundation of all values. The existence of a value depends upon the individual's recognition of something valuable. Values are revealed within the free act; they are not created in contemplation. That which is other than consciousness may make demands upon the individual consciousness; however, it is the individual freedom that determines by a free act whether or not a particular demand will be acknowledged as such.

> It follows that my freedom is the unique foundation of values and that *nothing,* absolutely nothing, justifies me in adopting this or that particular value, this or that particular scale of values. As a being by whom values exist, I am unjustifiable. My freedom is anguished at being the foundation of values while itself without foundation.[30]

In the freely chosen relation by which being-for-itself seeks to establish its own being, there always exists a lack. For human consciousness is always becoming and never quite *is*. This lack is value.

One of the functions of existential psychoanalysis is to reveal to the individual the moral nature of his being. The individual is thereby made aware of the fact that it is by his own act that values come to exist.

> It is then that his freedom will become conscious of itself and will reveal itself in anguish as the unique source of value and the nothingness by which the *world* exists.[31]

[30] *Ibid.,* p. 38.
[31] *Ibid.,* p. 627.

To "reveal" to an individual his situation is the limit to which an existential psychoanalysis can go. It remains for the individual himself in the act of free choice to accept his situation and the anguish by which it is revealed. In so doing, the individual chooses to exist authentically.

What absolute freedom prescribes by way of an ethical principle is nothing more than the acceptance on the part of an individual of his freedom by means of his own free choice. The continual reaffirmation of this principle produces an authentic existence. However, for a person to accept his freedom may not be as simple a matter as it may first appear. In choosing an authentic existence, a person rejects all sources of values other than his own consciousness and rejects all values not revealed through his own acts. Authentic existence is, then, not a simple matter of attitudes or beliefs, but it is a way of life. It is a life of active choice-making, and its authenticity is a matter of the quality of the person's actions. The quality of an action is determined by whether or not the individual chooses his action upon a free choice made in the anguish that arises from the knowledge and acceptance of the choice as ungrounded and unjustifiable. It is also made in the anguish that arises from the realization that the person is fully responsible for the consequences of his action.

> For I declare that freedom, in respect of concrete circumstances, can have no other end and aim but itself; and when once a man has seen that values depend upon himself, in that state of forsakenness he can will only one thing, and that is freedom as the foundation of all values. That does not mean that he wills it in the abstract; it simply means that the actions of men of good faith have, as their ultimate significance, the quest of freedom itself as such.[32]

The second feature of existential ethics is derived from what might be determined the objective side of the individual's commitment to free choice. Because of the existence of others, whose freedom the individual freely posits, the individual is responsible for all others. The individual's free acts involve him not only in a responsibility for creating himself, but also impose upon him the responsibility for creating humanity itself. Although an individual's purpose may be strictly personal, it has a "universal value." The purposes of humanity may not coincide with those of the individual; still, none are wholly foreign to the individual, for the purposes of the individual are always presented or chosen in relation to the purposes of humanity: either as an attempt to surpass, to deny, or to adapt to them. In making the choice, the individual thereby contributes to the change, denial, or acceptance of "universal values" or goals.

---

[32] Jean-Paul Sartre. "Existentialism is a Humanism" in *Existentialism from Dostoevsky to Sartre,* selected and introduced by Walter Kaufmann (New York: Meridian Books, 1956), p. 307.

What is at the very heart and center of existentialism is the absolute character of the free commitment, by which every man realizes himself in realizing a type of humanity—a commitment always understandable, to no matter whom in no matter what epoch—and its bearing upon the relativity of the cultural pattern which may result from such absolute commitment.[33]

Sartre's ethics, then, not only place absolute responsibility upon the individual for what he is and becomes, but also insist that he is equally responsible for what human society is and becomes. Norman Greene summarizes Sartre's ethical position as:

. . . the obligatory pursuit of chosen ends, accompanied by a constant awareness that they are freely chosen and that a new choice is possible. It requires both action and uncertainty, activity and reflection, modes of life which have often been held to be incompatible.[34]

Contrary to the popular impression of the affective nature of existential ethics, it appears more justifiable to conclude along with Professor Greene that Sartre's ethics require a rational assumption of the human condition:

. . . that an individual is most likely to move in the direction of the integration of his personality and the progressive realization of his goals if his efforts are based on a rational understanding of the human condition.[35]

Such a conclusion is acceptable only if it is clearly understood that the "rational" is not being used in the eighteenth century philosophical tradition of Rationalism. Rather, it should be understood that by a "rational assumption" Sartre would more nearly mean the *conscious and deliberate* acceptance of the human condition. This assumption of the human condition produces the authentic way of life. That such a way of life is possible for all is attested by the universality of the human condition. The experience of anguish through which the absolute freedom of the individual is revealed is an experience available to all, and "the assumption of freedom is open to all."[36]

[33] *Ibid.*, p. 304.
[34] Norman N. Greene, *Jean-Paul Sartre: The Existentialist Ethic* (University of Michigan Press, 1960), pp. 56-57.
[35] *Ibid.*, p. 58.
[36] *Ibid.*, p. 59.

chapter 3

From Absolute Freedom
to Education

INTRODUCTION

Making the transition from the philosophy of existence to education is couched with difficulties. The central cause of these difficulties lies in the fact that few major existentialists have seen fit to direct their attention directly to the area of education. Jean-Paul Sartre is certainly no exception. His nonphilosophical concerns lie in the adult realm of social and political crises, rather than in the area of educational issues. Thus, Jean-Paul Sartre provides no true guide for the interpretation of existentialism for educational applications. To relate the meanings implicit in Sartre's notion of absolute freedom to the matter of curriculum theory will be difficult, to say the least. However, it is hoped that such an undertaking, which is the purpose of this chapter, will provide less general and ambiguous results than attempts made to relate existentialism in general to education in general.

Ralph Harper and George Kneller are two scholars who have made serious attempts to relate this philosophy of existence to the area of education. Because of the rather wide divergence among existentialists' views, the efforts of both Harper and Kneller to deal with existentialism as such have led them to conclusions that are inconsistent with the views of Jean-Paul Sartre in particular and possibly inconsistent with the views of a number of other existential thinkers as well.[1] Such conclusions tend to create a false impression of existentialism, particularly in connection with its relation to education. Rather than deriving the educational implications directly from particular existential views, both Harper and Kneller appear to be concerned with indicating that existentialism is really consistent with at least most of the educational aims, if not prac-

---

[1] Ralph Harper and George Kneller are used in this chapter only as two examples of the danger inherent in any overgeneralization concerning philosophic positions and/or ''schools.'' A number of other authors might have served this purpose equally well.

tices, prevalent in the United States. It will suffice to remark that such an undertaking has a tendency to distort the philosophical concepts under consideration by deriving at least part of their meaning from "foreign soil." As mentioned in the previous chapter, existentialism is clearly in the tradition of European philosophy. It would appear dangerous at best to justify an indigenous institution of one society by a philosophy clearly in the tradition of another culture.

However, the purpose in introducing Harper and Kneller at this point is to make use of their writings in trying to directly infer the educational implications of existentialism.[2] Like existential analysis, or human consciousness itself, the most effective method or function is that of negation. Some of the conclusions reached by Harper and Kneller will be cited in the following pages for the purpose of showing, first, what Sartre doesn't mean by "knowledge" and "knowing" in relation to education, and second, what Sartre doesn't mean by "authentic existence." Following this rather negative excursion, the remainder of this chapter will be devoted to an exploration of the "remains" of the "absolute freedom" and the determination of whether or not enough is left to make any significant contribution to the theory of curriculum.

KNOWLEDGE AND EDUCATION

It will be recalled that for Sartre all knowledge is intuitive. It is directly appropriated by the individual in the free act of selection by his consciousness. In a sense, knowledge exists only as personal knowledge; it is "my knowledge." Knowledge, then, is a creation of individual freedom. It is difficult to reconcile this position with some of the conclusions drawn by Ralph Harper concerning the relation of existentialism to education. Consider the following:

> This is why it is not empty exhortation for existentialism to encourage individuals to know themselves and their time. The existentialist believes that there are certain things, certain truths, which every man ought to know, and which he has all too little time to know.[3]

From what source, it must be asked, is the "ought" derived? Every man's freedom is absolute; it is ungrounded. It cannot be from human consciousness that the obligation arises. Perhaps what man "ought to know" is himself. But a man is nothing except his acts. What does it mean to

---

[2] Ralph Harper, "Existence and Recognition," in National Society for the Study of Education, *Modern Philosophy and Education* (Chicago: 54th Year Book, Part 1, University of Chicago Press, 1956), pp. 215-258. And George Kneller, *Existentialism and Education* (New York: Philosophical Library, Inc., 1958).

[3] *Ibid.*, pp. 227-228.

say "I acted without knowing it"? For a man to know himself as free makes equally little sense. Man is freedom and most men spend a lifetime trying to escape this condition. It is not something that needs to be accepted. To suggest that the act of knowing carries out the many obligatory sanctions certainly seems to contradict both Sartre's notion of absolute freedom and his view of knowledge as intuitive. It seems more plausible to consider that nothing but the individual's own freedom can compel the act of knowing. The freedom of others is not in itself a determining factor in judging what "ought" to be known.

Another of Professor Harper's conclusions runs as follows:

> The world and truth are for him to explore, but they are also for him to commit himself to as one commits one's self to a community which not only permits freedom but enlarges the self.[4]

The first part of this statement implies that the world and truth or knowledge exist as independent entities and that it requires man's exploration to reveal both. This ignores Sartre's dictum concerning the individual, for "he is the one by whom it happens that *there is* a world."[5] A more accurate statement might read: the world and truth are for him to *create*. Further, to be committed to "one's self" is to be committed to the world and truth. For a person to be committed to his freedom is to be committed to the free acts by which such freedom is expressed, and it is by these free acts of the individual that there is a world, truth, community, and so forth. To suggest that a community can "permit" freedom or "enlarge the self" is again to deny the absolute nature of freedom. The only limit to freedom is freedom itself. What may be more accurately considered here is that an individual who is committed to himself—that is, his freedom—will, in fact, be committed to the world and truth, committed by virtue of the fact that they are his creation and are his responsibility, totally and absolutely.

Professor Harper also draws the conclusions that:

> Both teacher and students must learn to recognize something between and at first—if not always—beyond them, the truth of the subject matter.[6]

Failing to provide a definite definition of "subject matter," Professor Harper's examples of algebra and social sciences must be relied upon to indicate what he means by this term. The word "truth" here presents no real problem, for if a subject matter becomes directly appropriated, that is, intuited, then it is appropriated "in truth"—unrelated to anything

4 *Ibid.*, p. 234.
5 Sartre, *Existentialism and Human Emotions*, p. 52.
6 Harper, *Op. Cit.*, pp. 250-251.

else in the world. However, a problem does arise when it is suggested that the subject matter is something common between or "beyond" the students and teacher. The very notion of the free act of knowing precludes the possibility of a common knowledge or subject matter. The point that should have been made here is that knowing constitutes a free act which provides an object to be intuitively appropriated by the individual. To appropriate or know another person is to limit his freedom; thus, in a classroom it would be more educationally suitable for individuals to know themselves or some object, rather than other selves.

A final conclusion taken from Harper's essay is as follows: "Education is immediately concerned with recognition, not decision or action."[7] Regardless of what Mr. Harper means by "recognition," it must be asked: can education be anything else *but* decision and action? Take, for example, the very nature of knowing itself. The knower must first decide, choose to know; this constitutes a conscious decision. Then, by an act or acts of nihilation the object to be known is set apart from all relations with other objects. Now, the knower is in position to directly intuit or *know* the object. There is no *knowing* without decision and action. Perhaps it might be argued that *knowing* is not the chief concern of education.[8] What then could it be? Living an authentic life? But an authentic life is judged by the quality of its acts, and quality refers to whether or not the act was the result of a free choice, or a choice freely assumed.

Turning now to the work of George Kneller, in an early summary statement he indirectly quotes Gabriel Marcel. The quotation provides an apt illustration of the danger of combining two or more existentialists under a single classification.

> As Marcel says, the challenge to education in this age is to guarantee an atmosphere of freedom in which the students are encouraged to seek and find factual bases for making decisions which are both significant and personal; . . .[9]

It is difficult to see just what Kneller has in mind when he makes the statement cited above. Just preceding this statement he asserts that "education must therefore concentrate on the freedom of the total inner being and this includes the acceptance of facts and data only insofar as they have significance for the individual."[10] "Total inner being" or being-for-itself is freedom. Just what it would mean for education to

---

[7] *Ibid.*, p. 253.
[8] Actually, Ralph Harper seems to mean by "recognition" the "act of learning." Cf. Harper, *Op. Cit.*, p. 252.
[9] Kneller, *Op. Cit.*, pp. 90-91.
[10] *Ibid.*, p. 90.

"concentrate" upon it is uncertain, but this possibly constitutes no serious problem in itself. However, what is more serious is how to reconcile this with Marcel's suggestion of "guaranteeing an atmosphere of freedom." Freedom does not exist anywhere other than as consciousness; to be conscious is to be free; nothing outside of consciousness can limit or expand freedom. An additional difficulty arises in connection with the "acceptance of facts." Here again Kneller seems to be presenting a view that would not appear to be necessarily inconsistent with the existentialism of Jean-Paul Sartre. But, to support such a statement with the indirect quotation of Marcel seems to render Kneller's whole point somewhat incomprehensible. Sartre would, of course, strongly deny that there can be any "factual bases for making decisions," and to "seek" for such bases constitutes an unauthentic act, a seeking to escape one's own freedom. It is not an easy task to derive educational implications from existential thinkers, and such a task is confounded by mixing the views of the various existentialists together "willy-nilly." It must also be reasserted that according to the Sartrian view, facts or knowledge cannot be sought as a basis for making decisions, for a free choice is without support.

Further along in his work, Professor Kneller maintains that "the treatment of subject matter in such a way as to discover its truth in free association"[11] is one of the goals sought by the teacher. The misleading part of this assertion from a Sartrian view of knowledge rests with the term "discover." To discover something generally implies that the "something" exists prior to any discovery. For Sartre, an undifferentiated world as such exists. But both subject matter (or knowledge?) and its "truth" are created by the free acts of individuals; they do not exist "universally" but only as an individual's creation. And, as indicated earlier, truth and knowledge are directly intuited; they are caused to appear and then are appropriated. In such circumstances, truth and knowledge are indistinguishable.

Finally, Professor Kneller arrives at the most amazing conclusion concerning knowledge and the curriculum, and he seems clearly to associate such a view with Jean-Paul Sartre. Consider the following quotations:

> The necessity of mastering certain fundamentals is defended by Sartre, not only in his statement that we must expect to learn from the judgment of others but because being situated is an essential and necessary characteristic of freedom . . .

> Here, then, is no question of which is the more important, pupil or curriculum, but one of commitment on the part of the pupil to the

[11] *Ibid.*, p. 116.

curriculum as it represents a world of knowledge for him to explore. There is no doubt about the *fact* of the binomial theory, the Christian Bible, the life of Abraham Lincoln; and such facts as are known should be mastered in order to provide solid content for uninhibited analysis and criticism, and to establish firm foundations for individual creative effort. It is through the curriculum as a respected body of knowledge that the student develops personal freedom and appropriate habits of mind; . . .[12]

In connection with the first part of the passage cited here, two questions must be raised. (1) What does ''learning from the judgment of others'' have to do with ''mastering certain fundamentals?'' (2) What does ''being situated'' have to do with ''fundamentals?'' Kneller fails to give any reference for the statement of Sartre's, so it will be necessary to infer a meaning for the statement and to indicate how this meaning is consistent with Sartre's general position concerning ''others'' and inconsistent with Kneller's interpretation. Learning ''from the judgment of others'' can mean only that a person recognizes the freedom of the other and recognizes it as a freely posited limit to his own freedom. ''Learning'' must refer to the recognition of the free acts of others as possible limits to the individual's freedom and to recognize them in order to bring the individual's free choices within the situation itself. That the ''judgment of others'' has something to do with fundamentals as a ''respected body of knowledge'' appears inconsistent with the role of ''others'' as described by Sartre as well as inconsistent with what Sartre means by ''knowledge.'' Further, ''being situated'' or more accurately ''being free only in situation'' is the universal condition of man. Therefore, it cannot have as a prerequisite any ''mastering of certain fundamentals.'' All persons are capable of experiencing their freedom; the only requirement is to be conscious, and this is not something to be ''mastered.''

In the second paragraph of the quotation, the difficulty that arises in connection with the term ''explore'' has already been outlined in the preceding discussion. Three of the implications that can be drawn from this passage and which appear contradictory to the existentialism of Sartre are: (1) freedom is acquired; (2) freedom develops in an individual; and (3) that existing external standards have determined ''appropriate habits of mind.'' First, man is freedom; hence there is neither necessity nor possibility of acquiring it. Bodies of knowledge, no matter how ''respected,'' are not in the least relevant to there being freedom in the world. Second, the individual's freedom cannot be developed due to the fact that it already exists in full. Recognition and acceptance is all that freedom requires from the individual. Third, there can be no *a priori* or objective standards determining ''habits of the mind'' or any

---

[12] *Ibid.*, pp. 123-124.

other habit or pattern of behavior. To suggest that commitment to the curriculum can produce either freedom or "habits of the mind" is totally inconsistent with Sartre's views. Even more, such a commitment would be an act of bad faith on the part of the individual. Commitment to one's self—to one's freedom—is the only authentic form of existence.

From the critical comments of the preceding pages, certain definite factors emerge in connection with the relation of Sartre's views of knowledge and education. The act of knowing is a free act on the part of the individual. As such, it cannot be maintained that knowledge itself is a prerequisite for freedom. An individual's knowledge is possible by virtue of the fact that he is free. As an act of free choice, knowing involves both decisions and actions, assuming that these might be separated to begin with. Insofar as knowledge arises in the act of knowing, which is composed of both deciding and acting, it cannot be considered an objective basis for making decisions. To so assume is to be involved in an infinite regress. Knowledge, arising out of an individual's free act, cannot appeal to any social standard for its justification. The determination of any obligation or "oughtness" concerning the acquisition of some specific knowledge is solely a matter of individual choice. Finally, as a result of the preceding criticisms, it is clear that commitment on the part of the individual to anything other than himself—his freedom—is an act of bad faith or an unauthentic act. The act of knowing reveals only knowledge of the self and the individual's own situation.

ETHICS AND EDUCATION

Ethics for Sartre is a matter of living an authentic life, a life in which acts of bad faith are avoided. Yet, here again, both Harper and Kneller make assertions meant to hold for all existentialists even though such assertions appear to be inconsistent with some of the basic notions of Sartre. For example, Ralph Harper maintains that "existentialism is concerned principally with liberal education, freeing man from his isolation and his anonymity, . . ."[13] In the "strict sense" this is, for Harper, the "end" or value of an existential education. Such an "education can point to the way or ways to both happiness and good character."[14] Through such statements, Harper clearly reflects the moral nature or tone of all existential thought. Also, it may clearly be inferred from Harper's statements that any education purporting to be consistent with existential views will constitute primarily a moral or ethical enterprise.

However, the specific moral implications of Harper's assertions are

[13] *Ibid.*, p. 227.
[14] *Ibid.*, p. 253.

not consistent with Sartre's views on ethics. To use the term "liberal" in its more traditional sense of "freeing" is completely contrary to Sartre's notion of freedom. Man is free; therefore, it makes little sense to speak of "freeing" him. What is morally or ethically required here is for an individual to confront and accept his freedom with all its attendant responsibilities. Furthermore, an individual's "isolation" is an indispensable part of his situation. To be free is to stand alone, to confront as individuals the necessity of making a choice without support or justification and to be solely responsible for the consequences without reprieve. The individual finds himself alone in a meaningless, absurd universe, and it is only through his freedom that meaning, values, and a world exists. The "anonymity" evidenced in modern mass societies is, for Sartre, only evidence of bad faith and inauthenticity. Anonymity results from the choice of individuals who try to escape their freedom. Hence, a man cannot be "freed" from his anonymity, for he has freely chosen it. He must simply choose himself and his freedom.

In its more common usage, the term "happiness" finds no place in the authentic life prescribed by Sartre. The best that can be hoped for in terms of reward, end, or goal showing authentic existence is the satisfaction and dignity that arises from the individual's assertion of his freedom in the face of an absurd universe.

> Zeus: What do you propose to do?
> Orestes: The folk of Argos are my folk. I must open their eyes.
> Zeus: Poor people! Your gift to them will be a sad one; of loneliness and shame. You will tear from their eyes the veils I had laid on them, and they will see their lives as they are, foul and futile, a barren boon.
> Orestes: Why, since it is their lot, should I deny them the despair I have in me?
> Zeus: What will they make of it?
> Orestes: What they choose. They're free; and human life begins on the far side of despair.[15]

Again, "good character" if used in its common manner implies some set of standards toward which an individual strives. However, for Sartre, like Orestes, the only goal toward which the authentic person, the person of "good character," strives is his self.

> Orestes: . . . You shall give me your hand, and we will go—.
> Electra: Where?
> Orestes: I don't know. Towards ourselves. Beyond the rivers and mountains are an Orestes and an Electra waiting for us, and we must make our patient way towards them.[16]

---

[15] Jean-Paul Sartre, *No Exit* and *The Flies,* translated by Stuart Gilbert (New York: Alfred A. Knopf, 1947), pp. 159-160.
[16] Sartre, *The Flies,* p. 161.

"Good character" can only be judged by the authenticity of the individual's actions. If Professor Harper has Orestes in mind as a person of "good character," then there is some merit in asserting that education can "point the way" to good character. It must be kept in mind, however, that "pointing the way" as Orestes does for Electra does not compel "the way" to be chosen. As in the case of Electra, it may be rejected.

George Kneller also fails to clearly identify the relation between education and existential ethics. Professor Kneller asserts that "the existentialist prefers to cultivate the affective side of man."[17] Yet Kneller recommends that the teacher become aware of human situations by means of analysis: "These situations should be analyzed in terms of their irrational as well as rational components."[18] In referring specifically to values, Kneller offers the following summary of Sartre's view:

> Sartre, on the other hand, believes that it is the individual alone who creates values—values which make the morass of man's experience both intelligible and meaningful to him. Fact and value therefore constitute an irresolvable dichotomy.[19]

The ambiguity of Kneller's statement seems to stem from his postulation of a dichotomy between fact and value, and between the affective and cognitive or rational side of man. It is difficult to find anything in the works of Sartre to justify such a dichotomy. It seems more consistent with Sartre's views to assert that in an authentic life no such distinction can be made, and where it is made it is usually done in an effort on the part of an individual to escape his freedom, an act of bad faith. Knowledge is intuitive, thereby requiring an act of free choice—an act made in anguish. Facts are determined by free choice, for in the act of choosing this fact rather than some other, its value is asserted, created. The possible source of confusion which arises in connection with this dichotomy may be in the term "rationality" or "rational." The rationalism of the eighteenth century is viewed by most existentialists as a form of "rationalization", that is, the creation of logical systems for the purpose of justifying some external reality, human nature, values, and so forth. In short, it becomes a form of bad faith or escape from freedom. However, this does not imply that Sartre or many other existentialists reject reason or rational behavior from the authentic life. Rather, if "rational" is taken as meaning "conscious and deliberate" when applied to acts or behavior, then the existentialism of Sartre must insist upon the "cultivation" of "rationality." "Conscious and deliberate" in existential terms imply the

---

[17] Kneller, *Op. Cit.*, p. 61.
[18] *Ibid.*, p. 59.
[19] *Ibid.*, p. 59.

total involvement and commitment of the individual; hence, there can be no division between man's affective and cognitive sides.

What then, can be concluded from this negative treatment of existential ethics? First, that it must be noted that man's absolute freedom precludes the existence of any standards or any external values by which he may guide his acts. Therefore, the purpose of existential ethics cannot be involved with the development of "good character." "Good character," if it means anything at all to the existentialist, refers to an individual's life which is being lived authentically, that is, in acceptance of the individual's absolute freedom. A second point that has emerged in connection with existential ethics is that man is his freedom and that the conditions of this freedom require that man stand alone and in isolation. Therefore, an existential ethic cannot be involved with the *development* of freedom, for man is free whether he will or not. What gives the moral tone to the authentic life, and hence is the basis of existential ethics, is the recognition and acceptance of man's absolute freedom. Finally, it must be noted that happiness cannot be a basis for existential ethics. The authentic life requires that the individual be prepared to pass to "the far side of despair." In so doing, man attains a sense of dignity which comes only by his assertion of his freedom in the face of an absurd universe. Therefore, in relation to education the ethics of Sartre must imply as basis values the authentic life and the recognition and acceptance of man's absolute freedom. The task of education would seem to be one of preparation, preparation to accept the human condition—a condition of absolute freedom.

ABSOLUTE FREEDOM AND EDUCATION

The concepts of absolute freedom and education raise a number of questions concerning the very possibility of establishing any relationship between the two. Consider, for example, the following questions.

(1) Is absolute freedom available to a child?

(2) Is maturity a prerequisite or condition of authenticity, that is, a prerequisite to the free acceptance of the human condition?

(3) Can education occur without free choice on the part of the student?

(4) Does not the very existence of a school "system" imply that human existence or nature can be defined?

These questions must be met before it will be possible to continue the consideration of the relation between education and freedom, and later in particular the relation of education to the curriculum.

Is absolute freedom available to the child? To deal with this question will require that an inference be drawn from the stated philosophical position of Sartre. To maintain consistency with Sartre's views, it will be necessary to assume that a child, so long as he is conscious, is free. However, the child can be free only in situation, that is, within a particular context. The child's situation would appear to be considerably different from the situation of an adult. The determination of just how the situation of a child would vary from that of a mature individual is yet to be made. This is not to imply that there is no existing research in the area of child psychology, but rather that such research does not at present deal with the topic in terms of Sartre's existential psychoanalysis. It must be assumed, then, that the child is absolutely free. At least one contribution that education might make in view of the child's freedom is to lead the child to become more fully aware of his situation.

Is maturity a prerequisite or condition of authenticity, that is, a prerequisite to the free acceptance of the human condition? In this connection, the acceptance of the human condition as such must await a degree of maturity. But again, the degree is yet to be determined. However, authenticity as the acceptance by an individual of *his* particular situation can be attained at varying levels of maturity. Here the role of the school would be that of bringing the child into direct confrontation with *his* particular situation.

Can education occur without free choice on the part of the student? The answer to this question must be "No!" on two counts. First, the intuitive nature of knowledge precludes the child coming to know something without his freely choosing to appropriate that which is to be known. Second, formal schooling itself must be freely chosen by the child. In other words, the notion of compulsory education would seem to be totally inconsistent with a Sartrian view.

Does not the existence of a school "system" imply that human existence or nature can be defined? Certainly such a question must be answered in the affirmative. Any system automatically determines or fixes some aspect of human existence. The implications of this position for education are clear. The existence of a *place of education* does not necessarily require that the content of education itself be systematized. It would seem, then, that an existential view of education would preclude any fixed organization or systematization of educational content.

What, then, can be said concerning the relation between education and absolute freedom? First, in connection with the problem of freedom and the maturity of the child, the school can better relate itself to the child by recognizing the absolute freedom of the child in relation to this particular situation. Also, the school must be prepared to recognize authentic choices on the part of the student when met in relation to the student's own situation. Second, the free choice of individuals, as well as the immature members of society, must be acknowledged both in the area of the acquisition of knowledge and in the commitment to education itself. Knowledge results only as an act of free choice, and such a free choice is most likely to occur when made within the larger context of the free commitment to education itself. In conclusion, then, the relation between education and absolute freedom may be said to be that of a free act of commitment to education on the part of the one to be educated. Absolute freedom further implies that the function of education will be primarily that of allowing the individual to confront his own situation.

ABSOLUTE FREEDOM AND THE CURRICULUM

The question that seems appropriate to ask concerning the relation of freedom to curriculum theory may be phrased as follows. What education would be relevant to the preparation of youth so that their development into knowledgeable and moral adults is assured? From the previous discussion of the relation of freedom to education, three propositions concerning education have emerged that may be considered as possible *aims* of education. First, formal education must be presented in such a way as to elicit a commitment on the part of each youth and to warrant a continuing commitment or continual recommitment by the youth. Schooling, then, must cease to be compulsory. Only by the free commitment to education by the individual to be educated can knowledge be had or the authentic life lived. A second aim of education consistent with Sartre's concept of absolute freedom is that the school should develop within each student the capacity of analyzing his own situation. It must be reemphasized here that little is known about the situation of the immature members of society as it would be described in existential terms. However, it would seem safe to assume that the individual's situation varies with increasing maturity. This might be evidenced by the change in the concept of self projected by the individual, as well as by the degree of awareness of the relevance of his "facticity" to the projected self. The third educational aim requires that schooling insist upon the student's acceptance of the full responsibility for and consequences of such analysis. The student must have every opportunity to become aware of the consequences that follow from his analysis, and he must become conscious of the fact that he alone is responsible for these consequences.

Now, relating these aims to a curriculum theory will provide a somewhat clearer view of just what they entail. First, it must be assumed that the initial commitment to education has been made. Such a commitment may be encouraged and sustained by the curriculum.

However, in a proper sense, it will not be part of the curriculum theory itself.

A curriculum theory based upon Sartre's notion of absolute freedom will consist of three basic ingredients. First, the child will have available to him training in the application of analysis to his own immediate situation. Second, the child will be encouraged to behave authentically, or in the negative manner, to refrain from acts of bad faith. Third, the child and the curriculum will be continually evaluated upon the resulting behavior pattern of the child. As an adult "is his acts," so too will the child be judged. However, the judging will not be by adult standards of behavior!

Turning now to the first *ingredient* of the curriculum theory, it may be asked, what is specifically involved in existential analysis? In terms of a secondary school curriculum, the following description would seem appropriate. First, the student would have the opportunity to confront a decision-making situation. By this is meant that the student would find himself involved in a situation in which he is required to make a choice.

Next, the student would be encouraged to analyze the situation. The analysis requires that the student become aware of the meanings given to his facticity by his proposed choice and how the choice reflects a previous freely posited end or project of himself. What can be demanded of the student in terms of his awareness of his facticity would seem to depend upon his level of maturity. For example, a student's facticity at a low level of maturity may only encompass "his place" and "his environment," while at a higher level of maturity it would include "his past" and "his fellow man." Only at a stage nearing full maturity will the student's "freedom" and "death" enter into his facticity.

Following the analysis, the student would be confronted with the meaning of his situation and himself as "being his" or even as "being himself." Revealing to himself that his free choice has given these particular meanings to himself and his situation, the student is faced with the further choice of accepting these as his or engaging in an act of bad faith in an attempt to escape the responsibility of his act. Thus, the moral aspect enters the education process. The escape from freedom is an easily detectable form of behavior. It would be the task of the schools to encourage authentic patterns of behavior, ones consistent with the situation of the individual at his particular level of maturity.

The final ingredient of an existential curriculum theory would be that of evaluation. The evaluation of all phases of schooling would be based upon the behavior patterns of those being educated. The basic criterion for evaluation would be the extent to which the school experience contributed to a change in the behavior of the student, and whether such changes resulted in more authentic behavior patterns for the individual student.

part Two

Inquiry and Education

chapter 4

A Theory of Inquiry

INTRODUCTION

If our modern era is noted as an age of science, then perhaps the ever increasing understanding of the method of science might be labeled as the prime factor in the rise of science. Certainly, since the time of Bacon, discussions and debates over the definition of ''scientific method'' or ''methods'' have occupied considerable time of both philosophers and scientists. Nor have the discussions of recent times been restricted to the domain of the physical sciences. ''Method'' and ''methodology'' have become terms basic to discussions revolving around the foundations of all areas currently demanding serious study. History, mathematics, and the social, behavioral, and biological sciences all are seeking to clarify and establish ''the appropriate method'' for pursuing knowledge within their specific areas. It might be noted that many of these areas seek their *identity* by means of the establishment of a special method—as opposed to the traditional approach of identifying and limiting an area of study by means of a formal definition.

It is to this situation that the second part of this work addresses itself. And, too, it is toward a clarification of this situation that John Dewey made an outstanding, if not one of his foremost, contributions.

> Dewey's philosophy begins and ends in logical theory as the method of *inquiry.* All of the many fields which this philosophy has explored are in terms of differences of subject matter variations upon the central theme of inquiry. A reciprocal relationship binds the theme and its variations: apart from the actual occurrence of the different kinds of natural events with distinctive qualities there would be no specific inquiries, much less inquiry into inquiries; apart from a generalized method of inquiry specific inquiries would lack direction and control.[1]

[1] Donald A. Piatt, ''Dewey's Logical Theory,'' *The Philosophy of John Dewey,* P. A. Schilpp, ed. (New York: Tudor Publishing Company, 1939), p. 109.

In this chapter John Dewey's concepts of "scientific method," "intelligent behavior," "reflective thinking"—or, for the remainder of this study—his "theory of inquiry" will be explicated. The first task will be to explain in just what sense Dewey equates "reflective thinking," "scientific method," "intelligent behavior," and "inquiry." Next, a somewhat detailed description of the various aspects of inquiry will be presented. Finally, the specific nature of scientific and social inquiry will be developed.

TERMINOLOGY

To understand fully Dewey's use of the term "inquiry" and how it becomes identified with such terms as "intelligent behavior," "scientific method," and "reflective thinking," it will be useful to refer briefly to what is often called Dewey's "naturalism." George Santayana summarizes the meaning of naturalism as "a primary system, or rather it is not a special system at all, but the spontaneous and inevitable body of beliefs involved in animal life, . . ."[2] If "patterns of behavior" were substituted for Santayana's "body of beliefs" in the foregoing statement, a more accurate picture of the starting point of Dewey's naturalism would be conveyed. For, "whatever else organic life is or is not, it is a process of activity that involves an environment."[3] Whether Dewey uses the term inquiry, reflective thinking, or some other, it is important to remember that he is not prescribing how such an activity *ought* to take place, based upon some exterior, *a priori* principle. Rather, he is interpreting a process of natural events, a particular kind of transaction that takes place between an organism and its environment. How Dewey derives the concepts of inquiry, reflective thinking, and scientific method from this transaction between organism and environment will now be briefly explored.

From the simplest organism to the most complex form of life, it is possible to observe and describe a common form of transaction between the organism and its environment. Such a transaction is often designated by the term "excitation reaction." By this Dewey means to describe singular events, that is, the occasion in which a specific excitation elicits a specific reaction. An example would be the specific reaction of a cutworm to the specific excitation of an electric shock. Such a reaction

---

[2] George Santayana, "Dewey's Naturalistic Metaphysics," *The Philosophy of John Dewey*, P. A. Schilpp, ed. (New York: Tudor Publishing Company, 1939), p. 245.

[3] John Dewey, *Logic: The Theory of Inquiry* (New York: Holt, Rinehart, and Winston, 1938), p. 25.

would have its correspondence in the higher organisms in such singular events as an eye-blink in reaction to bright light, or a knee-jerk to a sudden pressure. This excitation-reaction relation between an organism and its environment, by its very specificity, is by no means a sufficient relation for the maintenance of life. An organism, in order to maintain between itself and its environment the sort of balance necessary for life, must do more than react to excitations received from the environment. To react is to create imbalance; to restore balance the organism must act. This reaction action is called a "response"; and the excitation that requires of the organism more than a reaction is called a "stimulus." Of course, in acting, the organism must act in relation to something, and this *something* can only be its environment.

The first thing to note about this second form of behavior is that it is an integrated behavior. In the case of excitation-reaction behavior, the specific source of excitation and the specific reaction can be pointed to. Even though such singular transactions between an organism and its environment may occasion the survival of the organism in a specific instance, a prolonged survival requires a response rather than a reaction. Stimulation is not specific, for it too involves not only reaction but subsequent action as well. The stimulus-response pattern of behavior is one designed to integrate the life function of the organism with its environment. The stimulus is not solely a feature of the environment but of the internal mechanism of the organism also. The response is not only derived from the stimulus, but includes behavior directed toward the environment. The point to be made here is that the stimulus-response pattern of behavior cannot be fully accounted for by the usual distinction between the organism and its environment. The stimulus resides, as does the response, in both areas. Rather than organism *and* environment, organisms must be thought of as *in* an environment—or that they are both integral parts of one and the same nature.

A second thing to note about the stimulus-response form of behavior is its sequential nature.

> Because behavior is in fact a function of the total state of the organism in relation to environment, stimuli are functionally constant in spite of changes in specific content. Because of this fact behavior is sequential, one act growing out of another and leading cumulatively to a further act until the consummatory fully integrated activity occurs.[4]

This stimulus-response behavior of organisms tends to possess a cumulative effect as well as a direction. Again, to let Dewey summarize the point:

[4] *Ibid.*, p. 31.

This integration is represented upon the organic side by equilibration of organic energies, and upon the environmental side by the existence of satisfying conditions. In the behavior of higher organisms, the close of the circuit is not identical with the state out of which disequilibration and tension emerged. A certain modification of environment has also occurred, though it may be only a change in the conditions which future behavior must meet. On the other hand, there is a change in the organic structures that conditions further behavior.[5]

To continue with Dewey's naturalism, it should be noted how Dewey relates the human behavior pattern of inquiry to the organic pattern of stimulus and response. Rather, it might be stated, this most basic form of organic behavior contains the basic components which in the complex behavior patterns of man form the basis of inquiry. For inquiry, as a specialized form of human behavior, arises out of a stimulus-response situation; that is, an unbalanced or disturbed state emerges out of a settled, balanced one. A response is then made toward a restoration of the balanced, undisturbed state. In such a process, inquiry constitutes a response in the sense that a change results in the conditions due to the action taken toward and upon the environment. The process—or pattern of inquiry—is sequential. This is merely to show here the relation of organic behavior to inquiry; the detailed analysis of the pattern of inquiry provided later in this chapter will clearly show this relation.

What has been important to note in the preceding few pages is, first of all, that Dewey's naturalism is one which places the organism and its environment as integral components of nature itself. Second, Dewey's description of the interaction and integration between organism and environment contains the ingredients out of which inquiry develops.

Still, man's environment does not consist solely of physical nature, but also of the social setting in which man finds himself. However, the social or cultural aspects of man's environment merely constitute an added dimension to his behavior patterns. Nevertheless, this dimension is one entirely unique in the domain of nature. Modern man derives most of his stimuli from other people, social institutions, symbols, and tools. In short, his environment is primarily social rather than merely physical.

Of distinctively human behavior it may be said that the strictly physical environment is so incorporated in a cultural environment that our interactions with the former, the problems that arise with reference to it, and our ways of dealing with these problems, are profoundly affected by incorporation of the physical environment in the cultural.[6]

This culturally transmitted environment in which man finds himself

[5] *Ibid.*
[6] *Ibid.*, p. 43.

immersed brings about "an incorporation within the physical structure of human beings of the effects of cultural conditions. . . ."[7]

The primary factor responsible for this "incorporation" of the "effects of cultural conditions" is language. Language, as such, is singled out as the primary factor on the basis of its being the most pervasive of the symbolic activities of man. As man's environment becomes increasingly dominated by social and cultural institutions, so the need to share common patterns of behavior increases. Organic behavior occurs in time, and in relation to a particular organism. In order for behavior patterns to be shared, as required in the case of social behavior, they must be both general and in a sense nontemporal. They must be general insofar as particular behavior must have a validity for persons other than the particular individual; the results of such singular instances of behavior must hold for all instances of similar behavior. Behavior patterns must be nontemporal, for the specific behavior occurs in time—its components are linked temporally—but the anticipatory results of others engaged in similar behavior is not linked temporally with the specific behavior. In short, language functions as the vehicle by which organic behavior can be formulated in such a manner as to render it general and nontemporal. Hence, language provides an essential tool for man's continued functioning as a *social animal.*

There are aspects of language which indicate both its continuity with organic behavior and its special function in man's transaction with his predominantly social environment. Besides being a cultural institution itself, language is:

> . . . (1) the agency by which other institutions and acquired habits are *transmitted,* and (2) it *permeates* both the forms and the contents of all other cultural activities. Moreover, (3) it has its own distinctive structure which is capable of abstraction as a *form.*[8]

Briefly, then, language by its general and nontemporal formulations of behavior is in a position to provide for the vicarious transmission of social behavior patterns from one person to another. In lower organisms the direct imitation of such patterns is the only means of transmission. Such vicarious transmission is facilitated by the fact that all social or cultural activities contain some symbolic form of linguistic activity as an integral part of the total. Finally, language is a distinguishable aspect of social behavior and, hence, itself transmittable as an essential tool in man's continuing transactions with his social environment.

Dewey summarizes our preceding brief discussion of language as follows:

> The importance of language as the necessary, and, in the end, sufficient

---

[7] *Ibid.*
[8] *Ibid.*, p. 45.

condition of the existence and transmission of non-purely organic activities and their consequences lies in the fact that, on one side, it is a strictly biological mode of behavior, emerging in natural continuity from earlier organic activities, while, on the other hand, it compels one individual to take the standpoint of other individuals and to see and inquire from a standpoint that is not strictly personal but is common to them as participants or 'parties' in a conjoint undertaking. It may be directed by and towards some physical existence. But it first has reference to some other person or persons with whom it institutes *communication*—the making of something common. Hence, to that extent its reference becomes general and objective.[9]

Now, why this apparent digression into language? Language, as a unique type of cultural institution, carries within itself the basic ingredients of intelligent behavior, reflective thinking, scientific method, and inquiry. Language in its broadest sense, is a necessary condition for the existence of the above mentioned, highly specialized forms of social behavior. The purpose here will be to show the degree of synonymity between intelligent behavior, reflective thinking, and scientific method that can be established by reference to language alone. Inquiry will be discussed in detail in the subsequent section where its relation to these other terms will be made clear. Scientific method will also be discussed later, so its treatment here will be brief.

Dewey indicates that intelligence or intelligent behavior refers to instances of direct behavior becoming indirect.

> It continues to be overt, but it is directed into channels of examination of conditions and doings that are tentative and preparatory.[10]

"Tentative and preparatory," or anticipatory, is the kind of behavior required in relation to a social environment, and language's general and nontemporal aspect provides the means for such behavior. In other words, the behavior pattern associated with the term intelligence has as a necessary component *indirect action*. Such action requires some use of symbols, usually language.

Dewey identifies reflective thinking as:

> . . . the kind of thinking that consists in turning a subject over in the mind and giving it serious and consecutive consideration.[11]

Certainly this constitutes the kind of behavior that can be labeled indirect action. Also, it must be allowed that the mind itself does not "turn over." Neither is an organic behavior "turned over." The "subject" "turned over" in the mind can only be a general, nontemporal representation of a behavior—a symbol or linguistic sign.

[9] *Ibid.*, p. 46.

[10] John Dewey, *The Quest for Certainty* (New York: G. P. Putnam's Sons, 1929), p. 223.

[11] John Dewey, *How We Think* (Boston: D. C. Heath and Company, 1933), p. 3.

Language, as mentioned previously, may be abstracted as a form. The particular form that a linguistic behavior pattern takes may be required of language, hence its form will vary accordingly. If language is required to have, in addition to the common activities from which it springs, meanings consistent with all other previously derived meanings, then this constitutes a "scientific language." In behavior patterns which may be called "scientific method," this consistency of language takes precedence over the form derived from social behavior. What occurs here is a further generalization of behavior. For the form of language used in scientific activities is one step removed from its cultural sources, and is more general and nontemporal.[12] "Scientific method" also signifies a behavior that is indirect and requires the use of language—although language with a special form.

Intelligent behavior, reflective thinking, and scientific method have been shown to be synonymous in the following ways. First, all refer to a behavior pattern in which action becomes indirect. Second, all require the use of symbols or language to produce the generality and non-temporality essential for indirect behavior. In the following section it will be shown how Dewey's theory of inquiry incorporates both intelligent behavior and reflective thinking.

THE NATURE OF INQUIRY

Before proceeding to a description of the various aspects or phases of inquiry, it will be helpful to make a few general comments concerning inquiry itself. Inquiry, as Dewey views it, refers to a particular mode of behavior. Dewey's theory of inquiry is a description of this particular behavior pattern, rather than a prescription of some idealized form of behavior. That people do in fact behave in such a manner is beyond dispute.

> The existence of inquiries is not a matter of doubt. They enter into every area of life and into every aspect of every area. In everyday living, men examine; they turn things over intellectually; they infer and judge as naturally as they reap and sow, produce and exchange commodities. As a mode of conduct, inquiry is as accessible to objective study as are these other modes of behavior.[13]

In order to identify this particular pattern of behavior, it is necessary to seek a behavior pattern common to such activities as judging, inferring, and examining. The point here is not that there can be only one form of behavior involving such activities, but that there is one pattern

---

[12] Nontemporal in the sense that the relation between subject and predicate is not temporally qualified.

[13] Dewey, *Logic*, p. 102.

of behavior that has proven itself to be most successful in dealing with these activities. There are many responses possible to the various social stimuli encountered daily; but, in the case of a particular situation there is but one pattern of response which tends to *work* or be successful.

> *Inquiry is the controlled or directed transformation of an indetermi-*
> *nate situation into one that is so determinate in its constituent distinc-*
> *tions and relations as to convert the elements of the original situation*
> *into a unified whole.*[14]

Inquiry, then, is the successful form of response. But to what sort of stimulus is this response particularly appropriate? It is this "indeterminate situation" that will be described next.

What are the special features of the unique kind of situation which provides the basis for inquiry? As previously mentioned, the situation is characterized by indeterminacy. It is indeterminate in the sense that it is "uncertain, unsettled, disturbed."[15] But the uniqueness is derived from the fact that the indeterminacy emanates from a specific situation. It is not indeterminacy in general of which Dewey speaks, for such general uncertainty or indeterminacy can only lead to random, overt behavior. Rather, it is uncertainty which is associated with a specific situation. "Situation," for Dewey, refers not to single, experienced objects or events, but to all aspects involved in a specific transaction between an organism and its environment. Dewey also wishes it clearly understood that the indeterminacy exists as a feature of the situation, not as something existing solely within our own heads or nervous systems. Uncertainties that are not related to an existing situation are symptoms of mental illness. It should be noted further that the resolution of an indeterminate situation occurs only with a modification of the situation itself. Hence, the disturbed, unsettled aspect of a situation cannot be said to be subjective. Mental processes alone cannot bring about a resolution.

> The biological antecedent conditions of an unsettled situation are in-
> volved in that state of imbalance in organic-environmental interac-
> tions . . .[16]

Nature, then, cannot be the source of indeterminacy. For it is only in the transaction between an organism and its environment that nature becomes an environment for an organism.

For the organism, the problem arising out of the unsettled situation is one of appropriate responses. What response or series of responses will modify the existential situation toward determinacy? For such a

[14] *Ibid.*, p. 104.
[15] *Ibid.*, p. 105.
[16] *Ibid.*, p. 106.

transaction between an organism and its environment to become inquiry, the initial responses must substitute indirect action for direct action, and reflective thinking must be possible.

The initial step in inquiry involves the recognition of the indeterminate situation as problematic and requires that the response be one of indirect action, rather than overt behavior. However, the mere recognition of a problematic situation is but a small move on the road of inquiry. Such recognition must lead to the statement of the situation in terms of a problem or problems.

> The way in which the problem is conceived decides what specific suggestions are entertained and which are dismissed; what data are selected and which rejected; it is the criterion for relevancy and irrelevancy of hypotheses and conceptual structures.[17]

Our conception of the problem, then, determines the future course of the inquiry. Notice here how quickly recognition has moved to statement. It is at this stage of inquiry that an existential situation (specific and temporal) has been transformed into a nonexistential one (general and nontemporal). For, it is only in this form that the "turning over" of reflective thinking can proceed. Hence, the linguistic or symbolic aspect of this step is inescapable.

A problem may be stated, but such a statement derives its meaning only insofar as the statement contains within it suggestions as to a possible solution or solutions. In order for these suggestions to contain *meaning* as possible solutions, they must also be derived from a statement of the problem which includes "the facts of the case." By "facts of the case" Dewey refers to those portions of the problematic situation that are relatively fixed. Of course, not all factors can possibly be fixed in an indeterminate situation. Further, suggestions arising from the statement of the problem acquire the label of "idea" only as they undergo examination as to their potential value as guides to the resolution of the problematic situation. Here, then, is an area or phase of interaction. It is a phase of inquiry which is controlled both by the statement of the problem and by the generation of possible solutions in terms of the problem.

Ideas themselves, once developed, require an additional dimension of meaning. This new dimension is attained by what Dewey calls "reasoning." Reasoning is the process of relating the meaning of an idea to other meanings in the same symbol system. This process results in making the original idea precise to a point whereby operations for application can be clearly ascertained and criteria for verification are developed. In general, by this method the applicability and verifiability of ideas are

[17] *Ibid.*, p. 108.

anticipated. It is clearly a symbolic activity; its success will depend to a large measure upon the consistency of the relationship between the various related meanings in the symbol system. However, without this reasoning process being carried out to some extent, indirect action comes to a halt and only direct action remains open as a behavior pattern. And,

> . . . since the latter terminates inquiry there is then no adequate inquiry into the meaning that is to be used to settle the given situation, and the conclusion is in so far logically ungrounded.[18]

While this process of relating the meaning of an idea to other meanings in the same meaning system is the hallmark of scientific method (a point to be elaborated in the subsequent discussion of scientific inquiry), it should be noted that it is also an essential phase of inquiry in general.

> Since this principle also applies to the meanings that are elaborated in science, the experimental production and re-arrangement of physical conditions involved in natural science is further evidence of the unity of the pattern of inquiry.[19]

It is interesting to note upon what basis the existential "facts of the case" and the nonexistential idea are able to relate in such a manner as to resolve an existential situation. For Dewey it is the operational character of both facts and ideas that make such "cooperation" possible. Ideas are operational in the sense that they function as a source and guide for further observations and operations. Facts are operational in the sense that they are capable of being organized in such a way as to enable them to function as evidence. Facts are of necessity selected—all facts cannot be included. The selection depends in part upon the quality of the indeterminate situation and in part upon which facts can be ordered in such a way as to serve as evidence.

To conclude this sketch of Dewey's theory of inquiry, then, let it be noted that inquiry is a process. It is a process that arises as a possible response to an existential situation, a situation characterized by its indeterminacy. It is a process that terminates in an existential situation; a situation characterized by its determinacy. Part of this process of inquiry involves the transformation of the initial existential situation into one which is nonexistential, from which in turn is derived the final existential situation. It is this nonexistential phase of inquiry that involves what Dewey terms intelligent behavior and reflective thinking. It is in this same phase that a response is channeled from direct action to

---

[18] *Ibid.*, p. 112.
[19] *Ibid.*, p. 118.

indirect action, and for Dewey, to intelligent behavior. This indirect action constitutes the provisional stage of inquiry. The provisionality of this stage is possible only through the use of language or symbols, for anticipatory judgments can be made only by means of generalization and in terms of anticipated time. Language possesses the characteristics of both generality and nontemporality. However, while this provisional phase of inquiry is general, nontemporal, and nonexistential, the process of inquiry itself is specific, temporal, and existential. The stimulus to inquiry arises out of a specific situation at a specific time. It concludes in a specific situation at a specific time.

SCIENTIFIC INQUIRY

In this section Dewey's identication of scientific method and inquiry will be explicated. There are two features of scientific inquiry that distinguish it from the general process of inquiry. First, scientific inquiry may be distinguished by the special nature of the language or languages that are employed. Ordered discourse and the transformations possible within such discourse provide the key to universal applicability of the results of scientific inquiry. However, this difference in subject matter is not one of kind, but of degree. The degree to which cultural influences directly affect inquiry constitutes the basis for separating science and nonscience. Problematic situations become the subject matter of science when the statements of the problem are made independently of direct cultural influences. This permits the process of inquiry to be controlled only by those ideas which operationally relate the statement of the problem to its possible resolution. These two features, as further described, will provide the connection between the general application of inquiry and scientific inquiry as employed in Dewey's theory of inquiry.

The linking of scientific inquiry and scientific method will be accomplished by describing how scientific inquiry incorporates within itself and successfully accounts for two age-old problems commonly associated with scientific method. These problems are the process of induction-deduction and the concept of causality. In addition, it will be shown how Dewey's notion of scientific inquiry resolves or dissolves the dichotomy between the pure and applied sciences—a seemingly inherent difficulty with most descriptions of scientific method.

The language of science and especially the role of ordered discourse and transformations in scientific inquiry will need to be examined more closely. The language of science, referring here principally to mathematics, but by no means exclusively so,

. . . is intrinsically free from the *necessity* of existential reference while at the same time provides the *possibility* of indefinitely extensive existential reference such as exemplified in mathematical physics.[20]

If we recall that the indirect action of inquiry or intelligent behavior requires the formulation of statements, it is not difficult to see how such statements are to be ordered. The initial statement is of the problem; subsequent restatements clarify the "facts of the case" until a statement is arrived at which clearly identifies the "facts" and contains an idea for operationally guiding the transformation of the indeterminate situation into a determinate one. The ground, or rather the degree to which the final statement is said to be *well grounded,* is determined by the extent to which the process of statement formulation is ordered. In the case of scientific inquiry, this ordering is accomplished by "a series of transformations conducted according to rules of rigorous (or necessary) and fruitful substitution of meanings."[21] A special language is required for such transformations. Such a language may be thought of in terms of the technical vocabulary of science, wherein concepts are rigidly controlled by formal or stipulative definition in such a way as to indicate their interrelatedness with other concepts within the particular science. But, more precisely, these requirements of transformation in scientific inquiry are exemplified in the symbol system of mathematics.

For Dewey, mathematics constitutes the best example of a symbol system that fulfills his first requirement of being "intrinsically free from the *necessity* of existential reference." Mathematics is not merely a higher order of abstraction, but abstraction of a different kind. The unique quality of this kind of abstraction lies in the fact that the ordering of discourse in mathematical symbols is accomplished solely with "reference to satisfaction of its *own* logical conditions."[22] Such "logical conditions" are themselves matters of abstract relationships and therefore are without existential reference. Hence, transformations within mathematics may be carried out indefinitely without reference to existential situations. A mathematical statement or proposition may undergo a series of transformations totally independent of any existential interpretation placed upon its contents or terms. As Dewey states it: "The contents of a mathematical proposition are freed from the necessity of any privileged interpretation."[23]

This very freedom of mathematical propositions provides the necessary condition enabling Dewey's second requirement to be met. The fact that existential reference is irrelevant to the ordering or transformation

[20] *Ibid.,* p. 394.
[21] *Ibid.,* p. 395.
[22] *Ibid.,* p. 396.
[23] *Ibid.,* p. 398.

of mathematical statements constitutes the condition that makes possible "indefinite extensive existential reference." Freed from any "privileged interpretation," such statements may be assigned an indefinitely extensive range of material interpretations or meanings. This enables the most general of generalities to possess at the same time the widest possible range of interpretations.

The role of mathematics in scientific inquiry is exemplary, first, because it clearly demonstrates a phase of inquiry in its most successful form. "Successful" here is used in the sense of providing the maximum control of inquiry. This control of inquiry is acquired through the ability of mathematical propositions to be transformed in accordance with rules governing the relationships between mathematical propositions and between their terms. To the extent that these transformations can take place without existential references they provide the inquirer with the possibility of control of application. The inquirer may provide existential content drawn from the "facts of the case" immediately at hand to the propositions.

Second, the role of mathematics in scientific inquiry is exemplary in that it constitutes the hallmark of scientific inquiry as compared with inquiry in general. Inquiry in general is a less successful form of inquiry because it is less controlled. The controllability of inquiry is directly related to the effective transformability of propositions within the process of inquiry itself. Scientific inquiry differs from ordinary inquiry in its degree of controllability—that is, the degree to which propositions may be transformed without existential reference.

Ordinary inquiry and scientific inquiry are often distinguished by the so-called difference in subject matter. For Dewey, "conclusions form a body of organized subject matter."[24] These conclusions are statements that express a final judgment upon the result of an inquiry. There are as many subject matters as there are situations that undergo the process of inquiry, but not all judgments resulting from inquiry are organizable. The chief basis upon which judgments become organized is their ability to function as aids to further inquiry. Thus, all judgments which culminate from inquiry, and which in turn promote and aid in subsequent inquiries, constitute an organized subject matter.

Scientific subject matter is composed of the results of scientific inquiry which are organized in such a way as to be usable in furthering subsequent scientific inquiry. The organized subject matter of physical science, for example, is notable for its fruitfulness in the promotion of continuing inquiries. This is not due to some inherent trait within the problematic situation dealt with by the physical sciences. Rather, this

[24] *Ibid.*, p. 463.

productiveness of the subject matter of physical science is fully accounted for in terms of the method of inquiry. It is the language of science, its transformability, and its effectiveness in the control of inquiry that sets off the subject matter of science from other organized subject matter. It is the ordered discourse possible within scientific inquiry that makes possible the tight organization of the conclusions of scientific inquiry. The productiveness of these conclusions is due to the abstractness of the ordered discourse which permits the widest variety of "privileged interpretations" and, hence, applications. Therefore, any problematic situation may be reconstructed into the organized subject matter of science. Whether or not the reconstruction takes place is determined by the method of inquiry employed. The extent to which the method is free of direct cultural influences and the degree to which ordered discourse and transformations are possible will determine the extent to which the reconstruction can take place.

To say that inquiry and scientific inquiry differ in subject matter is to say only that the methods of inquiry differ. The difference lies in our ability to make more effective use of ordered discourse in some inquiries than in others. The reasons for this ability have been indicated briefly and will be fully explored in the subsequent section dealing with social inquiry.

Before proceeding to this discussion, there still remains the matter of clarification of the identification of scientific inquiry and scientific method. This will be done by indicating how scientific inquiry incorporates what generally has been meant by scientific method, and in addition how it resolves some of the difficulties associated with attempts to define scientific method.

The process of induction-deduction is one that must be accounted for in any attempt to deal adequately with scientific method. Modern science is often distinguished from the science of medieval and ancient times by its emphasis upon the inductive phase of its method. "Going from the specific to the general" has been, since the time of Francis Bacon, the identifying activity of the experimental method of modern science. The position that the essence of scientific method lies in the ultimate reducibility of scientific activity to the process of induction by simple enumeration is still widely held by philosophers of science.

> The task of science has been to infer from the observational material the general principles that are made of symbols and connected by logical operations.[25]

[25] Phillip Frank, *Philosophy of Science* (Englewood Cliffs, N.J.: Prentice Hall, Inc., 1957), p. 301. For similar statements see: Hans Reichenbach, *The Rise of Scientific Philosophy* (Los Angles: University of California Press, 1951), p. 229ff.; and W. H. Werkmeister, *The Basis and Structure of Knowledge* (New York: Harper and Bros., 1948), p. 261ff.

Inductive inferences are indispensable to scientific method,

> . . . because it is not the inference from the theory to the facts, but conversely, the inference from the facts to the theory on which the acceptance of the theory is based; and this inference is not deductive, but inductive. What is given are the observational data, and they constitute the established knowledge in terms of which the theory is to be validated.[26]

If Dewey had accepted this description of induction, then his notion of scientific method would have been reducible—as was Professor Reichenbach's—to a calculus of probability. Now, while the scientific activities of certain physicists do involve the kind of processes describable by probability calculus, other activities which are also classifiable as scientific are not so describable. Furthermore, this restrictive notion of induction would seem to preclude any continuity between the behavior describable as general inquiry and scientific inquiry. Thus, it was incumbent upon Dewey to provide an adequate description of the inductive process that could be applied to the broader range of activities classifiable as inquiry, to the activities of scientific inquiry, and to scientific method.

What Dewey rejects is the idea that "observational data" are given. If such data were given, then what criterion could be used to determine when an adequate amount or number of data had been acquired? How many specifics justify a generalization? Clearly, the variation is a wide one. This problem disappears when data are considered *not* as given, but as being themselves a product of inquiry.

> The inductive phase of the inquiry consists in the observational and experimental operations by which we work over crude symptoms and refine them so that they indicate meanings.[27]

The "meanings" that are relevant to the inductive phase of scientific method are those that lead to the institution of "a case that is *representative* of various phenomena in such a way that it warrants a general proposition."[28] The *mystery* of how to progress from specifics to the general is thus disposed of. Specific data are selected in such a way as to justify the general statement. Data are sought to determine whether or not the case is typical. Data become the facts of inquiry only within or during the process of inquiry itself. Once a case is established as typical, then only this one case is needed to justify an inductive inference.

For an inductive inference to have complete meaning, it must go

---

[26] Reichenbach, *Op. Cit.*, p. 230.

[27] Donald A. Piatt, "Dewey's Logical Theory," *The Philosophy of John Dewey*, P. A. Schilpp, ed. (New York: Tudor Publishing Co., 1939), p. 129.

[28] Dewey, *Logic*, p. 479.

beyond the mere statement of the ''facts of the case.'' It must also indicate and provide means of verifying proposed solutions. Proposed solutions are stated as hypothetical ''if-then'' propositions. Such formulations involve the process of deduction, the asking of what is implied in the general statement. This process, if conceived as ''going from general to specific,'' is misleading. To ask for the implication of a proposition is to ask for implied meanings. Only meanings are deducible from meanings, and all meanings are general. The deductive phase of scientific method provides direction for action, observation, and verification.

> The development in discourse of the directive conception that is involved provides the sole verifiable material for identifying the deductive phase of scientific method.[29]

To the extent that scientific method involves the processes of induction and deduction, Dewey's concept of scientific inquiry is identifiable with scientific method. However, scientific inquiry not only accounts for induction and deduction, but it provides a description that frees these phases of scientific method from some of their traditional ''difficulties.''

Since the time of David Hume, the notion of causality or ''laws of causality'' has been an issue with which philosophers of science and describers of scientific method have felt compelled to deal. The satisfactory account of causal relationships or of the ontological status of ''causal laws'' has eluded the philosopher of science. Yet somehow, scientific method seems dependent upon this very notion. For Dewey, every completed inquiry involves causal propositions. Causal propositions are also involved in scientific inquiry and share with the various concepts of scientific method a need for justification.

John Dewey places the notion of causality within the behavioral context of inquiry. ''Every intelligent act involves selection of certain things as means to other things as their consequences.''[30] The category of causation is a linguistic or logical means by which inquiry is given direction.

> To bring about, to produce, to make, to generate, is to effect, and that which serves this purpose is a cause in the only legitimate existential sense of the word.[31]

Statements expressing a causal relation are actually, upon analysis, descriptions of the relation of means to consequences. For example, consider the statement, ''Green apples cause stomach-ache.'' Green apples,

---

[29] *Ibid.*, pp. 432-433.
[30] *Ibid.*, p. 460.
[31] *Ibid.*, p. 461.

the subject term of this proposition, creates a disposition on the part of the hearer to seek within the subject for this thing called "cause." However, if the statement is put in terms clearly showing cause as a means-consequence relation, then there is little temptation to seek an explanation of cause in either the subject or predicate term. Such restatement may be put this way: if a stomach-ache is desired, then the eating of green apples can bring about this condition. Thus, the "legitimate" use of causal propositions permits their translation into a hypothetical deductive form, and in such a form their function in the direction of inquiry becomes evident.

The notion of scientific laws, such as causal laws, is treated in a similar manner by Dewey. Scientific laws are those propositions which are used to control and direct a wide range of scientific inquiries and which have done so successfully over a period of time. It is not uncommon for objects to be given labels that signify their potential uses rather than their particular content. Hence, "causal laws" like "gravitational laws" are terms designating potential consequences of certain classes of activities. They are not terms designating some ontological element.

Causation and causal laws, long deemed essential to scientific method, are shown by Dewey to be an integral part of scientific inquiry. They are shown to function as directors and controllers of inquiry. They serve this function as logical categories; that is, they described the means-consequence relationship between elements of a possible existential situation.

A final point relating Dewey's concept of scientific inquiry and scientific method is that of the contrast between so-called pure and applied science. The generalizations or laws of science are without meaning until they are provided with a "privileged interpretation," and such an interpretation can be drawn only from an existential situation. The generalization must be applied. Furthermore, the generalizations of science must have been themselves abstracted from existential situations. To limit science to the establishment of generalizations is to rule out the very lifeblood of science itself: experimentation.

> Nothing so fatal to science can be imagined as elimination of experimentation, and experimentation is a form of doing and making. Application of conceptions and hypotheses to existential matters through the medium of doing and making is an intrinsic constituent of scientific method. No hard and fast line can be drawn between such forms of "practical" activity and those which apply their conclusions to humane social ends without involving disastrous consequences to science in its narrower sense.[32]

[32] *Ibid.,* p. 439.

SOCIAL INQUIRY

If all intelligent behavior in response to indeterminate situations is to be accounted for within Dewey's theory of inquiry, then a description of social inquiry consistent with the previous description of inquiry will need to be given. Inquiry as an individual response to indeterminate situations can readily be acknowledged as a constructive behavior pattern. The more refined version of inquiry, scientific inquiry, possesses a history of accomplishment and success to justify its claim as a desirable pattern of behavior. The method of social inquiry, however, finds itself in a far less enviable position. Social inquiry does not appear to have produced many significant accomplishments in dealing with the various social problems that beset mankind. Its successes are described at best as modest. An individual has the opportunity to experience the successes that accrue by means of intelligent behavior when applied to personal problems, but at the same time he is unable to deal in a similar fashion with the larger social problems that perplex him. A description of social inquiry will not only need to be made in terms of the theory of inquiry, but will also need to account for its lack of success in terms of its failure to meet the logical requirements of inquiry itself. In the following pages, then, social inquiry will be placed within the context of the theory of inquiry. Following this, it will be shown that the "retarded" state of social inquiry, as compared to scientific inquiry, is due to its failure to meet the logical requirements of inquiry itself, and is not due to any inherent differences in subject matter.

If social inquiry is to be fitted into the context of inquiry in general, it must share the same origin. This origin must be none other than the stimulus provided by an indeterminate situation. Such indeterminate situations are existential, specific, and temporal. It is only from such a stimulus that a genuine problematic situation, the first step in inquiry, is generated.

> In fine, problems with which inquiry into social subject-matter is concerned must, if they satisfy the conditions of scientific method, (1) grow out of actual social tensions, needs, "troubles"; (2) have their subject-matter determined by the conditions that are material means of bringing about a unified situation, and (3) be related to some hypothesis, which is a plan and policy for existential resolution of the conflicting social situation.[33]

The recognition of a problematic situation involves the formulation of a statement or proposition. This statement may undergo a number of restatements or modifications. The final statement of the problematic

[33] *Ibid.*, p. 499.

situation includes the ''facts of the case.'' That scientific inquiry deals with ''the facts, all the facts, and nothing but the facts'' has been shown inconsistent with the actual state of affairs in science. The selection of facts occurs in all types of inquiry. The successful experiences resulting from scientific inquiry have had a cumulative effect upon the widening circle of scientific inquiries, so as to provide the scientist with fore-knowledge of some of the kinds of facts relevant to the successful reso-lution of a particular kind of problematic situation. It is clear that social inquiries are not so provided. Does this imply that social inquiry must begin with all the facts, or with an arbitrary selection of facts, or with no facts? By no means! The facts relevant to any inquiry are selected in and by the process of inquiry itself. An immediate basis for the selection of the ''facts of the case'' that suggests itself is the identification of those factors which appear as barriers or obstacles to the satisfactory reconsti-tution of the indeterminate situation. Also, those factors which may provide positive resources for the institution of a determinate situation may be identified and selected as ''facts of the case.'' The *trouble* with social inquiry is that the ''facts of the case'' are not so easily obtained, for social situations are not static. Perhaps the success of scientific in-quiry is due to the stability of its indeterminate situations. It should be noted that the situations dealt with in science are far less static than they were fifty years ago, and this has not impeded the progress of scientific in-quiry. What inquiry requires of social situations is the recognition that change does and will take place. What are to be selected as ''facts'' are those elements which can serve to control the direction of the change. Inquiry itself is a process designed to bring about a change. If the subject matter of inquiry is undergoing change independently of in-quiry, then the chief problem of inquiry is to affect a control over the direction of change. Hence, the ''facts of the case'' are to be selected on this basis.

The next phase of inquiry is the development of an idea, or the conceptual subject matter. This phase involves the ordering of the ''facts of the case'' in such a way as to suggest an idea or concept that accounts for the facts, directs further observations, and suggests possible opera-tions to bring about the resolution of the indeterminate situation. Here too, the idea or concept is formed within and by the process of inquiry itself. As a result, the conceptual subject matter takes on the status of a hypothesis which serves to control and direct the process of inquiry and which may be revised in the light of existential consequences. The form-ing of this conceptual subject matter proves more difficult in social in-quiry than in scientific inquiry. In particular, the use of mathematical symbols facilitates this phase of inquiry in the sciences, for the ''privi-leged interpretations'' can be selected solely from the context of the inquiry itself. In social inquiry the symbolic forms with which the ideas must be expressed often contain "privileged interpretations," or meanings derived from outside the inquiry. Thus, there is a tendency to introduce into social inquiry direct cultural influences, prejudices, and the like, even though such factors are external and irrelevant to the inquiry. The success of social inquiry will depend to a large extent upon the development of symbols that will render built-in cultural influences less directly influential in the control of inquiry.

Inquiry makes a difference. That is, the consequences of inquiry are existential, and the difference they make determines the validity of the process of inquiry. In the case of scientific inquiry the consequences are determined and the process verified by experimentation in a laboratory. Is this final phase of inquiry possible in social inqiury? Certainly there are more practical difficulties involved in the process of social inquiry. Dewey refers to "associated activities"[34] as one practical difficulty in determining the consequences of social inquiry. Associated activities include such matters as the securing of agreements and cooperation that are necessary for the required activity. However, such requirements are contained within the idea of any proposed solution.

> The idea that because social phenomena do not permit the controlled variation of sets of conditions in a one-by-one series of operations, therefore the experimental method has no application at all, stands in the way of taking advantage of the experimental method to the extent that is practicable.[35]

Finally, scientific inquiry and social inquiry need to be placed in the broader context of inquiry itself. "All inquiry proceeds within a cultural matrix which is ultimately determined by the nature of social relations."[36] In scientific inquiry the influence of the particular culture is only indirectly felt. Nevertheless, the kinds of problems that will concern the scientist are culturally determined by such factors as the general concerns of the cultures, the economic resources available for scientific inquiry, and the available technologies for experimentation. In turn, scientific inquiry results in changes in existential situations and therefore exerts a considerable influence upon the culture. Modern transportation and communication are just two areas of contemporary American culture that are direct results of scientific inquiry.

In the case of social inquiry the influence of the physical environment cannot be ignored. The human factor cannot be the sole concern of social inquiry. Social problems arise out of social relations which in

---

[34] *Ibid.*, p. 502.
[35] *Ibid.*, p. 509.
[36] *Ibid.*, p. 487.

turn are directly influenced by the physical conditions existing at the time. Such *physical conditions* are meant to include all physical elements within an environment from geography to industrial hardware. Social problems, then, arise out of existential situations and "In the broad sense of 'natural' social sciences are, therefore, branches of natural science."[37] Why, then, are the social sciences in such a backward state as compared with other natural sciences?

> The question is not whether the subject-matter of human relations is or can ever become a science in the sense in which physics is now a science, but whether it is such as to permit the development of methods which, as far as they go, satisfy the logical conditions that have to be satisfied in other branches of inquiry.[38]

To examine some of the causes for the failure of social inquiry to meet the logical requirements of inquiry, the phases of inquiry will be considered independently. First, there is the tendency on the part of social inquirers to manufacture problematic situations in the abstract, rather than forming the problem out of existential situations. This is to proceed upon the assumption that inquiry begins with a definite, well-defined problem, and that the process of inquiry consists solely in determining the specific means of solution. Such an assumption precludes the exercise of control in inquiry. It provides no basis for deciding what *really* is a problem, and it provides no basis upon which the derived operations can have any clear existential relevance. It becomes an exercise in futility. The problematic situations of social inquiry must derive their terms from specific indeterminacies arising within existential, social relationships in order to insure that the proposed operations will actually effect a change in the initial situation. To begin inquiry with a problem is to reduce the process of inquiry to a matter of simple deduction. Deduction in and by itself provides neither direction nor control for inquiry.

The establishment of the "facts of the case" is another phase of social inquiry in which the logical requirements of inquiry are not met. In their desire to attain the status of "science," the social sciences have tended to join Francis Bacon in the emphasis upon induction as the chief mode of inquiry. Many social scientists conceive of their job as being that of collecting the "facts of the case" and drawing generalizations therefrom. In order that their sciences may be objective, the social scientists work at freeing their inquiries from all value judgments and evaluations. The inductive requirements of inquiry make it clear that inquiry does not begin with the "facts of the case," but rather that the "facts of the case"

---

[37] *Ibid.*, p. 487.
[38] *Ibid.*, p. 487.

are determined in and by the process of inquiry. Induction, for Dewey, is not the *collection* of facts, but the *selection* of facts. Facts are selected in such a way as to warrant a generalization. Instead of collecting *all* the facts, the theory of inquiry requires the selection of *certain* facts. Such a selection involves an evaluation. Valuations are required in all inquiry. The basis for evaluations is not arbitrary, but determined in and by the process of inquiry itself and is continually subject to revision.

The phase of inquiry involving the formulation of the conceptual subject matter or ideas is also a phase whose logical requirements are neglected in social inquiry. Instead of constructing these ideas out of the ''facts of the case'' and in such a way as to suggest further observations and operations, there is a tendency in social inquiry to select ready-made ideas. The introduction of factors external to the inquiry in progress is fatal to any attempts to control inquiry. Ideas, like the ''facts,'' must be selected and developed in and by the process of inquiry itself. Furthermore, ready-made ideas introduced into inquiry from outside are not themselves subject to the control of inquiry. Justification of such ideas then tends to be made on some absolute standard or on the basis of inherent values. Under such conditions it becomes impossible for these ideas to attain the status which is logically required by the theory of inquiry, namely, the status of hypotheses. The difference between scientific and social inquiry on this matter is illustrated by the kinds of discussions that are carried on in each area. Discussions concerning social inquiries usually revolve around the intrinsic truth or falsity of some idea. On the other hand, discussions about scientific inquiries generally have to do with the effectiveness of differing operations or means of obtaining certain consequences.

The failure of social inquiry to meet some of the logical requirements of inquiry accounts for the retarded state of the social sciences. It is not to be denied, however, that the social sciences do encounter a large number of practical difficulties in any attempt to institute controlled inquiry. Rather than deter inquiry, these difficulties should serve as a stimulus to inquiry. One practical difficulty not previously mentioned is that of the increasing compartmentalization of the social sciences. Dewey's theory of inquiry provides no logical reason for such splintering, for neither subject matter nor method possess any inherent differences. An indeterminate situation arising from social relationships cannot always be stated as a problem in economics, or politics, or sociology alone. Compartmentalization can impede the adequate formulation of the problematic situation and its subsequent resolution. In conclusion, it should be noted that there is no logical difference between the sciences and the social sciences. The essential process of inquiry is the same and subject matters vary only to the extent that controlled inquiry is actually pursued.

In concluding this section on Dewey's theory of inquiry, it is well to be reminded that the various methodologies springing up in the contemporary scene reflect the division among human purposes and values.

> The effective condition of the integration of all divided purposes and conflicts of belief is the realization that intelligent action is the sole ultimate resource of mankind in every field whatsoever.[39]

Furthermore, John Dewey's description of intelligent action and inquiry is a major contribution to the possible resolution of the pressing problems of a scientific age.

> It cannot be repeated too often that experience is not a veil coming between man and nature, that it is a relation between organisms and environment which is itself natural and existential, that what is experienced is not simply more experience but a natural and real world. At the same time it must be understood that a man cannot know what he doesn't inquire into, that a forever unknown and unknowable reality is just that, and that calling "the world and truth the bright goals of free men" must mean—if anything at all—the giving of value to the stimuli and purposes of human inquiry. Dewey's contribution here—the idea of the solidarity of experience with nature and of knowledge with search—is crucial, not only for grasping a man's philosophy but for understanding the whole temper of a scientific age.[40]

[39] John Dewey, *The Quest for Certainty* (New York: G. P. Putnam's Sons, 1929), p. 252.

[40] George R. Geiger, *John Dewey in Perspective* (New York: McGraw-Hill Book Company, 1958). p. 84.

chapter 5

From Inquiry to Education

INTRODUCTION

Before applying Dewey's theory of inquiry to education and to curriculum theory, it would seem appropriate to offer some words of justification for such an application. First, it should be noted that Dewey's theory of inquiry constitutes the core of his philosophy. Not only is the theory of inquiry derived directly from Dewey's naturalism; but as Professor Piatt says, "Dewey's philosophy begins and ends in logical theory as the method of inquiry."[1] As indicated in the preceding chapter, inquiry is descriptive of a wide range of human behavior—man's behavior in relation to his physical environment and his behavior in relation to his social environment. To the extent, then, that the theory of inquiry may be considered as a philosophy, so the theory of inquiry may be said to be a "general theory of education."

> If we are willing to conceive education as the process of forming fundamental dispositions, intellectual and emotional, toward nature and fellow men, philosophy may even be defined as *the general theory of education.* Unless a philosophy is to remain symbolic—or verbal—or a sentimental indulgence for the few, or else mere arbitrary dogma, its auditing of past experience and its program of values must take effect in conduct.[2]

Second, inquiry as the basis of a general theory of education might seem to restrict education to intellectual factors and ignore the social and esthetic factors. But for Dewey, even though every subject can be intellectual, it is intellectual "in its function—in its power to start and direct significant inquiry and reflection."[3] Dewey further acknowledges that:

[1] Piatt, "Dewey's Logical Theory," *The Philosophy of John Dewey*, p. 109.
[2] John Dewey, *Democracy and Education* (New York: The Macmillan Company, 1961), p. 328.
[3] Dewey, *How We Think*, pp. 46-47.

. . . education is not exhausted in its intellectual aspect; there are practical attitudes of efficiency to be formed, moral dispositions to be strengthened and developed, esthetic appreciations to be cultivated. But, in all these things there is at least an element of conscious meaning and hence of thought. Otherwise, practical activity is mechanical and routine, morals are blind and arbitrary, and esthetic appreciation is sentimental gush.[4]

Inquiry, then, is important to all factors of education. As a reminder of the significance of inquiry or reflective thinking, Dewey's own words provide the best source:

. . . thinking enables us to direct our activities with foresight and to plan according to ends in view, or purposes of which we are aware. It enables us to act in deliberate and intentional fashion to attain further objects or to come into command of what is now distant and lacking. By putting the consequences of different ways and lines of action before the mind, it enables us to *know what we are about* when we act. *It converts action that is merely appetitive, blind, and impulsive into intelligent action.*[5]

Therefore, to the extent that "intelligent action" is desirable in all phases of education, the application of Dewey's theory of inquiry to the development of curriculum theory is justified.

In the remainder of this chapter, John Dewey's theory of inquiry will be used as the basis for developing a curriculum theory. First, the theory of inquiry itself contains criteria for theory development and will, therefore, be relevant to the discussion of the nature of curriculum theory in general. Second, the relation of inquiry to intelligent behavior in all parts of education makes inquiry a prime factor in determining the content of any curriculum theory. Each of these two applications of Dewey's theory of inquiry will be dealt with in turn.

THE NATURE OF CURRICULUM THEORY

The first step in dealing with the nature of curriculum theory is to have clearly in mind Dewey's concept of theory. There are several criteria that must be met before a judgment attains the status of theory. The first criterion is that theory must be the result of an inquiry. The formulation of this result takes place along the lines previously laid down in the theory of inquiry. In short, this result of inquiry is a proposition which contains the "facts of the case" as derived or selected from the indeterminate situation. It also contains the idea or hypothesis which provides direction and control for the process of inquiry. When this

[4] *Ibid.*, p. 78.
[5] *Ibid.*, p. 17.

proposition becomes a part of an assertion which is made at the termination of inquiry and which states both the "facts of the case" and the hypothesis, and in addition, indicates the outcome of the inquiry, it now becomes a judgment. This judgment or warranted assertion that concludes an inquiry is the *raw material* out of which theories are built. But as inquiry begins and ends in an existential situation, so then the raw material of theory must begin and end in an existential situation. This leads to the next criterion.

If a judgment is to attain the status of theory, then a judgment once formed must serve as a hypothesis in subsequent inquiries. That is, a judgment must be applicable to more than one problematic situation. So, judgments that terminate inquiries must either prove successful in subsequent inquiries or be modified towards adequacy. For a warranted assertion to become a theory, it must be continually subject to further inquiries.

Finally, the status of theory is conferred only upon those judgments which prove themselves fruitful in the suggestion of further inquiries. As an idea must serve as a director of further observations and as a prescriber of operations, so a theory must lead onward to new inquiries and suggest new problems. On the negative side, theory can never serve as a deterrent to further inquiry.

These criteria resolve the dichotomy of theory and practice so prevalent in most discussions of theory.

> Theory separated from concrete doing and making is empty and futile; practice then becomes an immediate seizure of opportunities and enjoyments which conditions afford without the direction which theory—knowledge and ideas—has power to supply.[6]

From these criteria it may be concluded that theories arise in the context of an inquiry. Theories are themselves subject to continuing inquiries and subsequent modifications. The ultimate evaluation of a theory is made on the basis of the theory's ability to produce further inquiries.

A second step in considering the nature of curriculum theory is to clarify Dewey's concept of education as a social function. For Dewey, it is by a process of continual self-renewal that society sustains and propagates itself. The maintenance of a society is possible only by means of introducing the immature members to its habits, institutions, and customs:

> . . . this renewal takes place by means of the educational growth of the immature members of the group. By various agencies, unintentional and designed, a society transforms uninitiated and seemingly alien beings into robust trustees of its own resources and ideals.[7]

[6] Dewey, *Quest for Certainty*, p. 281.
[7] Dewey, *Democracy and Education*, p. 10.

How is this educational growth possible? It is possible in the same manner as learning takes place in any organism. It is the ability of an environment to elicit certain responses in the individual that enables this transformation to take place. Man's environment is primarily social. That is, man's activities are to a large extent dependent upon the activities of other men; and a social environment is educative. It is educative insofar as mere training is insufficient to initiate the young into the rites, rituals, functions, and operations of a society. To insure the maintenance of the society, the young must be capable of sharing in the purposes and goals of the society itself. To the extent that the young are born into and are a part of society from the very beginning, they will in fact be educated. The social environment is then by its very nature educative.

Education as either schooling or formal education is viewed by Dewey as a special form of man's social environment. For various reasons, then, formal education is conceived of as a true function of society. It is essential to society in that modern civilizations have become too complex for the young to totally assimilate. It therefore requires that the elements of society that are to be transmitted must be identified and reduced into simpler components. In this process, society is able through formal schooling to eliminate undesirable factors in society. Bad habits or undesirable social traits can be eliminated from this special environment which is a school. In addition, it is possible through formal education for society to provide a balance of factors which are deemed essential to the continued growth and development of society. It is possible then to remove from those elements that are to be transmitted, factors which stand in the way of continuing social growth.

> The deeper and more intimate educative formation of disposition comes, without conscious intent, as the young gradually partake of the activities of the various groups to which they may belong. As a society becomes more complex, however, it is found necessary to provide a special social environment which shall especially look after nurturing the capacities of the immature. Three of the more important functions of this special environment are: simplifying and ordering of the factors of the disposition it is wished to develop; purifying and idealizing the existing social customs; creating a wider and better balanced environment by which the young would be likely, if left to themselves, to be influenced.[8]

If theory is not a notion posited for some reason extraneous to the process of inquiry, but is developed in and by continuing inquiries, then any theory of the curriculum will also need to be developed in the same manner. Acceptance of Dewey's view of education[9] as a social function

---

[8] *Ibid.,* p. 22.

[9] For the remainder of this book, the term education will be used to refer to schooling or formal education.

leads to the conclusion that any curriculum theory consistent with the theory of inquiry will be the result of social inquiries. It will be productive of continuing inquiries and will be subject to revision on the basis of the conclusions of such inquiries.

The nature of curriculum theory will be determined by social inquiry. Although the method of social inquiry was presented in the preceding chapter, there are several important points of which it will be well to be reminded. First, there is the specific indeterminate situation from which all inquiry springs and in which all inquiry ends. Next, there are the practical difficulties that confront the social inquirer, particularly that of terminating inquiry by experimentation. This is, of course, one of the key difficulties facing all educational inquiry. Finally, it is well to be reminded at this point of the open-ended nature of all inquiry. All warranted assertions or judgments must subject themselves to restatement as hypotheses for verification in subsequent inquiries. How does each of these points affect the nature of curriculum theory? Each will be considered in turn.

What then are the indeterminate and problematic situations from which inquiry springs and which produce a curriculum theory? The situation confronting anyone seeking to construct a curriculum theory is the necessity of selecting from a confused and confusing mass of social aims and goals those appropriate to education. The current proliferation of conflicting curriculum theories and attempts at imposition suggests that the problem of the selection of the aims of education has been made on the basis of their *a priori* or intrinsic worth. In terms of the theory of inquiry, these ideas or aims have been introduced from outside the process of inquiry, and, while a curriculum theory can be deduced from them, its relevance to existential situation becomes a matter of chance. Aims in education as properly viewed are:

> . . . suggestions to educators as how to observe, how to look ahead, and how to choose in liberating and directing the energies of the concrete situations in which they find themselves.[10]

The function of aims in education is to provide a particular position from which educational problems can be viewed with regard to further observations and subsequent resolution. They are in a sense "working hypotheses."

For aims to have value in education, they must meet the same criteria as ideas in the process of inquiry. They "must be founded upon the intrinsic activities and needs . . . of the given individual to be educated."[11] Thus, there can be no single aim in education. The aims must

---

[10] Dewey, *Democracy and Education*, p. 107.
[11] *Ibid.*, pp. 107-108.

be transformable, that is, capable of symbolic transformations so as to suggest concrete operations consistent with them. And, aims as verified by inquiry are never to be taken as final or ultimate; but they must be suggestive of other problems in which they may serve as hypotheses and be again subject to verification.

Dewey offers an illustration of the "problem of aims in education." Both nature and society have at various times asserted themselves as *the* basis for educational aims. The conflicts arising between the two positions are due to the restrictive view of nature produced by aims that posited physical capacities, including the mind, as the function of education. Or else, this view placed nature in direct opposition to society, and social institutions are thereby deemed "unnatural." The restrictive view of society places the subjugation of the individual to social control as the primary aim of education. The limitation of such aims is clear. Inquiry is a natural process and a natural pattern of behavior for man. Man lives by means of his environment. Man does not live to inquire, but inquires in order to live. But for man, inquiry takes place in an environment that is predominantly social. If rather than "social control" the "cultivation of power to join freely and fully in shared or common activities"[12] is given as an educational aim, then such a "power" is nothing less than intelligent behavior or inquiry. Thus, the positing of ideas external to inquiry produces aims that are conflicting and irrelevant to the actual problems of education. But, seen from the larger perspective of inquiry, these ideas become integrated.

The practical difficulty that besets the inquirer who addresses himself to the nature of curriculum theory and the aims of education is that of terminating his inquiry in an existential situation. The accomplishment of an experiment is far easier in a laboratory than in a social institution such as the school. However, it may be that this difficulty is due to a tendency to establish aims that are too general and have universal applicabilities. This tendency can be corrected only by insistence upon the procedure that requires aims to be generated from specific existential situations. By such a procedure an aim becomes clearly relevant to some specific situation and is testable by means of its capacity to suggest operations to bring about the desired change in the situation. Control and observation of results are a much greater possibility in limited, specific situations as opposed to larger, more complex ones. The possibility of the experimental testing of an aim is far greater in a situation involving a child and a teacher than in a school-wide situation.

Another practical difficulty that restricts social inquiry is that of direct cultural influences. Ideas, in order to control and direct an inquiry,

---

[12] *Ibid.*, p. 123.

must be produced in and by the process of inquiry itself. Yet, if such ideas contain ready-made meanings which reflect cultural biases, prejudices, and customs, then the specific problematic situation loses its control over the process of inquiry, and the results of inquiry prove irrelevant to the situation. Natural linguistics are, of course, products of their respective cultures; and they tend to preserve indiscriminately the full range of meanings assigned by the culture. If natural language is the best means of formulating the ideas of social inquiry, the difficulty is an important one.

The difficulty is by no means insurmountable. The resolution lies, however, outside the method of social inquiry. It lies rather in the attitudes which accompany the will to employ the method. In a somewhat different context Dewey describes the attitudes relevant to proper employment of his theory of inquiry.[13] One of these attitudes appears especially relevant to the solution of the difficulty of direct cultural influences. The attitude is labeled by Dewey as ''open-mindedness.'' By open-mindedness he means:

> . . . freedom from prejudice, partisanship, and such other habits as close the mind and make it unwilling to consider new problems and entertain new ideas . . . It includes an active desire to listen to more sides than one; to give heed to facts from whatever source they come; to give full attention to alternative possibilities; to recognize the possibility of error even in the beliefs that are dearest to us.[14]

The final point of the open-mindedness of social inquiry has considerable effect upon the nature of curriculum theory. It removes the possibility of curriculum theory taking on a fixed formal structure. Curriculum theory is composed of a set of hypothetical guides to the resolution of specific curriculum problems. As a guide, curriculum theory is evaluated by its effectiveness in leading to resolution of the specific problems. But, too, as the problems change so must the curriculum theory be modified to provide a continuing set of working hypotheses for their solution.

THE CONTENT OF CURRICULUM THEORY

The discussion of curriculum theory in the preceding section indicates that it is the nature of curriculum theory to acquire a related set of judgments which are the result of an inquiry or inquiries and provide working hypotheses for further inquiry. The continuing inquiries pro-

---

[13] Dewey, *How We Think*, pp. 29-33.
[14] *Ibid.*, p. 30.

vide the actual content or subject matter of curriculum theory. In order to deal more adequately with the content of curriculum theory, a distinction will be made in the following pages between those results of continuing inquiry that bear upon the overall organization of the curriculum and those that relate to the more specific content or subject matter of the curriculum. To continue the explanation of the relation of Dewey's theory of inquiry to curriculum theory, it will be necessary to limit the following discussion by establishing inquiry as an educational aim and by allowing it to function as the sole aim. The following discussion will also be limited by restricting the scope of curriculum to include only those features appropriate to secondary schooling. The importance to human society of inquiry or reflective thinking as a pattern of human behavior has been previously characterized. However, two contributions of inquiry will be mentioned here by way of summary.

First, it is through the process of inquiry that man gains increasing control over his physical environment. Physics is a prime example of the mushrooming effect of controlled inquiry. Modern physics is typified by chain reaction, not only the chain reaction of fissionable matter but of inquiry as well. In physics one inquiry does not lead to another but to several others, which in turn are multiplied many times. Such a chain reaction often carries inquiry beyond the field of physics itself and into many and varied sciences and technologies. And each inquiry brings with it an increased control over the physical environment.

Second, inquiry is a process by which man is able to share in the meanings which are his culture and by which he is able to contribute to their continued growth. In such a process the individual finds his own life growing in meaning. Any pattern of behavior other than inquiry terminates this growth in some final or absolute meaning. Man's growth as a man is a growth in and with a society, and to date inquiry is the only sort of transaction that guarantees its continuation.

The value of inquiry to human life is clear. But before establishing it as an educational aim it will need to be shown to what extent inquiry requires training. It has been indicated that inquiry is a behavior pattern natural to man. If this is the case, then why is any education required? Inquiry is indeed a natural pattern of behavior; however, this kind of behavior is often employed only in connection with acquiring the basic necessities of life. Some sort of training is required in order to insure the employment of inquiry beyond this limited range of stimuli. Man will naturally inquire into the making of fire where it is important to his survival and his comfort. But inquiry into the nature of heat and combustion requires the application of the process of inquiry to problems beyond the immediate necessities of life.

Training in the method of inquiry is further required to prevent the incorrect learning of inquiry and the development of bad habits or incomplete inquiry.

> While the power of thought, then, frees us from servile subjection to instinct, appetite, and routine, it also brings with it the occasion and possibility of error and mistake. In elevating us above the brute, it opens the possibility of failures to which the animal, limited to instinct, cannot sink.[15]

Where the requirements of life demand, inquiry is naturally controlled; but wherever these requirements are not involved there is a temptation to release the control. This occurs either in connection with failing to derive the problem from an existential situation or failing to test conclusions by application to the existential situation. Also, cultural influences are allowed direct access into the process of inquiry, and ideas are adopted with their meanings fully established beforehand. It is possible to accept many varied and even conflicting descriptions of situations so long as the description makes no real difference to the immediate conduction of life. For example, it makes no difference to the conduct of the average man's life today whether or not space is filled with ether or is a vacuum. Yet, controlled inquiry into the matter has provided physicists with judgments which have lead to new theories and which in turn have produced many practical social consequences for the average man. A noncritical acceptance of either view of space would have closed the door on possible further inquiries.

Another point must be made in connection with the need for education in the method of inquiry. The mere teaching of a method will not by itself prove adequate. Along with the method, education must provide the desire or will to employ the method to all indeterminate situations, rather than those of immediate concern. This desire or will is manifested in certain attitudes which insure proper employment of the method of inquiry. Dewey labels these attitudes "open-mindedness," "wholeheartedness," and "responsibility." By open-mindedness Dewey means:

> Freedom from prejudice, partisanship, and such other habits as close the mind and make it unwilling to consider new problems and entertain new ideas.[16]

By wholehearted Dewey means:

> When anyone is thoroughly interested in some subject or cause, he throws himself into it; he does so heartily, as we say, or with a whole heart.[17]

---

[15] *Ibid.*, p. 23.
[16] *Ibid.*, p. 30.
[17] *Ibid.*, p. 31.

And finally, responsibility for Dewey is:

> . . . to consider the consequences of a projected step; it means to be willing to adopt these consequences when they follow reasonably from any position already taken. Intellectual responsibility secures integrity; that is to say, consistency and harmony in belief.[18]

The great importance and relevance of inquiry to human society has been indicated, as has the necessity of including inquiry within the function of education. It now remains to ask whether or not inquiry can be included as an aim of education. Can inquiry be taught? Dewey indicates that there are several resources that are available to make the teaching of inquiry practicable.[19]

The first of such resources is that of the child's natural curiosity. Curiosity is a natural factor related to the acquisition of the "facts of the case" in inquiry. Its expression stems from a surplus of energies in the organism and is used up in activities of testing and exploring. In the small child, curiosity is often expressed in the random motions of reaching, groping, probing, and feeling. As the child develops, social stimuli come to play a part in his expression of curiosity. His curiosity is able to find satisfaction in the appeal to other persons for answers to the repeated question, "why?" Curiosity finally becomes manifest in the intellectual process of inquiry when the child develops sufficient interest in finding out for himself. This interest provides the degree of motivation required for the child to sustain his curiosity long enough to proceed to satisfaction by means of intermediate steps. The intermediate steps involve the use of objects as tools, acts as operations, and ideas as suggestions of further operations and educational goals. Thus, from the natural curiosities of a child there emerges the basic ingredients of inquiry. For this natural surplus of energy to be finally and habitually expressed as intelligent behavior, guidance and direction of all these is required. And guidance and direction certainly fall within the domain of education.

A second resource which adds to the practicability of making inquiry an educational aim is that of suggestion. The spontaneous flow of ideas that pass through a child's head whether he wills or not are deemed suggestions. Properly speaking, they become ideas when they become useful, that is, when they lead on to other ideas or activities. The task of education is to create situations in which useful suggestions are elicited, situations in which the natural random flow of suggestions becomes productive of ideas. Suggestions may be considered in three dimensions according to Dewey.[20] These dimensions provide the teacher with a

---

[18] *Ibid.,* p. 32.
[19] *Ibid.,* pp. 35-52.
[20] *Ibid.,* p. 42.

means of evaluating a child's response to a situation designed to elicit ideas.

The first dimension is that of ''ease and promptness.'' The ease and promptness with which a child responds often indicates the alertness and brightness of the mind. However, this is not always the case, for thinking things out requires time. The second dimension is that of ''range and variety.'' Too great a flow and variety of suggestions can deter a child's response by requiring choices among conflicting suggestions. On the other hand, too few suggestions limit the range of meaning which the child will be able to extract from the situation. The third dimension is that of ''depth and profundity.'' Regardless of the ease and variety of suggestions, some will deal directly with the key meanings of the situation while others will deal with only the most superficial meanings. The task of the teacher is not merely to create situations that elicit suggestions, but to bring them forth in the appropriate dimensions.

The third resource making inquiry a practical educational aim is orderliness. The flow of suggestions implies some ordering of the suggestions, even if this ordering means no more than an association of ideas. Inquiry, however, requires more than this.

> Only when the succession is so controlled that it is an orderly sequence leading up to a conclusion that contains the "intellectual force" of the preceding ideas, do we have reflective thought. And by intellectual force is signified force in making some idea worthy of belief; in making it *trust*-worthy.[21]

This requirement creates difficulties as well as opportunities for education.

> The absence of continued motivation cooperates with the inner plasticity of the immature to increase the importance of educational training and at the same time magnifies the difficulties in the way of finding consecutive modes of activities that may do for the child and youth what serious vocations and functions do for the adult.[22]

The opportunity for education lies in the fact that orderliness can be included as an educational aim only when presented in such a way as to make it justified in the immediate situation of the child. Yet, at the same time this habit of orderliness is a direct preparation for intelligent adult behavior.

Having shown the value of inquiry as an educational aim, and that it is not impractical to so establish it, the next topic to be considered is how inquiry as *the* aim of education serves as a key to the organization of the content of the secondary curriculum. Dewey's theory of inquiry

[21] *Ibid.*, p. 47.
[22] *Ibid.*, p. 50.

provides three organizational principles. Inquiry or intelligent behavior begins in the transaction between an individual and some indeterminate situation, and proceeds by abstraction to ideas which in turn suggest a course of action to be applied to the initial situation. Thus, all curriculum content should be organized so as to provide for the active engagement of the student. The content of the secondary curriculum must also be organized in such a manner as to provide the linguistic tools essential for the formation and transformation of ideas. And finally, the content must provide for observation, observation sufficient to allow the "facts of the case" to be identified, and sufficient to allow recognition of the results of inquiries. Each of these principles will be discussed individually in the following pages.

The first organizing principle comes from Dewey's notion of inquiry as being an active process or a pattern of human behavior. If the secondary curriculum is to be organized on the basis of inquiry, then whatever else the curriculum content might be it will be organized to involve the students actively. "Action is the means by which a problematic situation is resolved."[23] The tendency of any human organism is to be active rather than passive in relation to the environment. Many active pursuits have been included in the secondary curriculum in recent times. These include such things as student government, science laboratories, courses in vocational training, music, dramatic arts, fine arts, and speech. The inclusion of these areas in the curriculum has been due to the recognition of the natural activity requirements of the students. Seldom, however, have such inclusions in the curriculum been made on the basis of activity as an essential part of the process of inquiry. The mere existence of a curriculum organized around activities is no guarantee that such activities will contribute to the development of intellectual habits, that is, habits of inquiry. The problem of the organization of the secondary curriculum is to base all phases upon active pursuits and to further insure that they actively involve the student in the process of inquiry.

What are some of the criteria that must be met by an activity in order to provide the necessary training in the process of inquiry? One such criterion is that of the interest of the student. The activity must be such as to totally attract the interest of the student. The interest, however, must be attracted by more than just the prospect of momentary excitement. It must actively engage the process of thought as well. The process of thought is elicited in any human organism by an indeterminate situation. Thus, for an activity to engage the student, the process of inquiry must contain an indeterminate situation by means of which the student's interest is attracted.

[23] Dewey, *The Quest for Certainty*, p. 244.

Another criterion that an activity must meet, if it is to provide the necessary training in inquiry, is that the activity must have an intrinsic worth. By this it is meant that the activity must be more than momentary fun. It must contain an intellectual challenge. The problematic situation must be important enough to the student to justify the expenditure of energy necessary to reach a solution. It should also be important in a larger context. It should be important to the overall growth and development of the student.

Still another criterion to be met by an activity is that it must arouse new curiosities and new interests in the student. As inquiry is a continuing process, so should be the activity in which a student is engaged. The involvement in any activity should lead the student to the development of interests in related and continuing activities. In inquiry, solutions are not final or absolute, but serve as a stimulus to new inquiry by means of raising new problematic situations, which in turn require a new sequence of activity. Finally, activities in the secondary curriculum will, if they meet the above criteria, involve a considerable span of time. The kinds of activities that provide for the training in the process of inquiry will be continuing activities, and the student must be provided with the time necessary to explore not only the activity at hand but the activities that suggest themselves in the process of the initial activity. The activities that constitute the secondary curriculum should not be cut up into small time blocks. The curriculum should provide adequate time for the full process of inquiry to run its course.

A second organizing principle to emerge from Dewey's theory of inquiry is that of language. The use of language provides the prime tool by means of which individuals pass from physical activity to intellectual activity. This includes learning, for it is clear that when learning takes place what is learned is not things or objects but meanings. The process of inquiry as an intellectual activity is dependent upon language, for it is through language that direct physical activity can become indirect and provide the means by which reflective thinking can take place. The problem that presents itself for the organization of the secondary curriculum is that of the transformation of the social and practical use of language to the intellectual use or the use of language in inquiry. In short, the secondary curriculum must be so organized as to provide the opportunity for training in the transformation of language in its social use to its intellectual use.

Such an organization of the secondary curriculum takes place within an activity. The initial use of language occurs when it becomes necessary for the student to transform an indeterminate situation into a problematic situation. It is not only necessary to observe the "facts of the case" in the indeterminate situation, but to state them in language as well. It is in the statement of the problematic situation that language takes on intellectual use. It is in the activity of transforming the indeterminate situation to the problematic situation that the opportunity for increased vocabulary occurs. The increasing need for new terms with which to identify the "facts of the case" provides within the process of inquiry itself the means of enriching language. In making the transformation from the problematic situation to ideas or hypotheses, the necessity arises for constantly increasing the precision of the terms. For it is only as the terms are made adequately precise that the idea can be productive of suggestions for further observation and operations. To proceed from an idea to these suggestions requires the ordering of language. The ordering of language again is dependent upon the precision of the terms.

The process of inquiry requires language or some symbolic forms. To organize the secondary curriculum in accord with the theory of inquiry is to organize it in a way in which language is most fruitfully developed. For language as required in the process of inquiry is also best learned by the individual engaged in the process of inquiry itself. The process of inquiry provides the opportunity to increase the student's vocabulary, to encourage the most precise use of terms, and practice in the ordering of discourse.

A third organizing principle derivable from Dewey's theory of inquiry is that of observation. The secondary curriculum is to be organized so as to provide for training in the skills of observation. For this to be possible the notion of observation as an end in itself must be rejected. When observation takes place, something is observed, but not every element of the object is observed. For observation to be effective certain elements are observed, and the elements which are, in fact, observed are determined by some purpose or end-in-view. This critical or analytic form of observation arises from a need growing out of an activity.

Any activity in which a student is confronted with an indeterminate situation provides an ideal source of motivation to observe. Before the indeterminate situation can be transformed into a problem, the situation must be observed in order to determine the "facts of the case." That is to say, the situation is observed with a view to ascertaining the factors relevant to the possible resolution of the situation. However, motivation or interest in observation does not cease here. Once engaged in the process of inquiry, interest switches from the indeterminate situation to possible solutions and new observations leading to an actual solution which is confirmed only by observation.

Observation is itself an activity; therefore, training in observation must take place as an activity. Interest in observing occurs in connection with a need which arises from within an activity. The process of inquiry itself requires the activity of observation. Also, the process of inquiry provides by means of the indeterminate situation the source of interest or need for observation itself. Thus, skill in observation is essential to skill in the process of inquiry, and engagement in the process of inquiry will result in training the powers of observation.

Turning now from Dewey's theory of inquiry as a basis for curriculum organization, the question of the specific curriculum content or the subject matter of the curriculum remains to be answered. That the method of inquiry is relative to the issue is clear, for as Dewey says: "Never is method something outside of the material."[24] Nor is inquiry antithetical to subject matter: "It is the effective direction of subject matter to desired results."[25] However, before relating subject matter to the curriculum, the nature of subject matter itself requires some discussion.

The tendency of many educators to consider subject matter as a fixed group of facts has led to the conception of the curriculum as a number of independent collections of facts to be learned. The means by which students are to acquire these collections of facts are in no way related to the collected facts themselves. The subject matter is common to both teacher and student: the teacher to convey, the learner to acquire. Such a view of subject matter is inconsistent with Dewey's theory of inquiry.

To clearly ascertain the role of inquiry in determining the nature of subject matter, it will be necessary to separate the use of the term subject matter as referring to the organized bodies of knowledge such as mathematics, chemistry, history, and so forth, from its use in reference to the content of the curriculum. Subject matter as organized bodies of knowledge is revealed by the method of inquiry to be undergoing constant change and never permanently fixed. The subject matter of physics has evolved over many centuries, and has evolved by means of continuing inquiries into the problems of the physical environment. Neither the problems nor inquiries show signs of terminating, and with each completed inquiry the organized body of knowledge of physics becomes modified to some degree. To claim to be teaching physics as a fixed subject matter is to deny that physicists are still inquiring into physical problems, and it is to deny that the method of inquiry is relevant to the organization of physical science.

What then is the relation of subject matter as organized bodies of knowledge to the curriculum? The organization of knowledge represents knowledge stored in its most useful form: "useful" in the sense of standing ready to serve in further inquiries. And knowledge as "warranted

---

[24] Dewey, *Democracy and Education*, p. 165.
[25] *Ibid.*, p. 165.

assertions'' is the product or goal of inquiry, which leads to the conclusion that subject matter itself represents the goal of inquiry. Increasing numbers of "warranted assertions" organized in an ever more useful fashion constitutes the aim of inquiry. And insofar as inquiry is an educational aim, so too must subject matter be an aim of education. This is to say that subject matter is something to be continually developed in the process of education, rather than acquired at a certain time.

Most important, however, is that subject matter provides an invaluable resource for the teacher. It provides the teacher with a guide for selecting those activities in which the students are to be engaged. Activities can be selected in part upon their intrinsic worth, that is, activities that involve the students in behavior patterns which will have future social value. Such activities will involve the students in the control and direction of activities to reach desired ends. Selected activities will require intelligent behavior or the process of inquiry as a response. A teacher without the resources of subject matter will not be in a position to select such activities as will both arouse the immediate interests of the students and provide practice in intrinsically valuable behavior patterns.

Subject matter, as used to refer to the content of the secondary curriculum when viewed in accord with Dewey's theory of inquiry, varies from the subject matter used as a resource by teachers. It is subject matter as student activities rather than subject matter as teacher resources. The subject matter of the curriculum is composed of those activities which lead the student toward the acquisition and use of organized bodies of knowledge. They are activities that meet the criteria of student interest, intrinsic worth, and arouse new interests. The specific nature of the activity will be determined by the teachers' own subject matter resources, or in a wider context, by society at large, for the intrinsic worth of any subject matter is socially determined. The actual function of making such a determination lies with the social inquiries which constitute the nature of curriculum theory itself.

The theory of inquiry can provide some interesting examples of the relation between the two concepts of subject matter. Taking subject matter as consisting of activities, it is the natural tendence of such activities to extend their boundaries or limits as they are initially observed. If these activities extend or overflow, the initial boundaries may acquire additional meanings. Any activity, then, potentially contains a wealth of meanings.

> Normally every activity engaged in for its own sake reaches out beyond its immediate self. It does not passively wait for information to be bestowed which will increase its meaning; it seeks it out. Curiosity is not an accidental isolated possession; it is a necessary consequence of

the fact that an experience is a moving, changing thing, involving all kinds of connections with other things.[26]

The quest for additional meanings or extension of meanings must take place in an ever widening context. The present immediate activity can have only limited meaning. However, such an activity does not need to have its meanings limited by the present time or by the immediate physical surroundings. A present activity may derive additional meaning from previous activities which are related to or have lead up to the present activity. The immediate physical surroundings may be indefinitely extended to include an ever wider physical setting in which the activity is occurring. Every activity may be said to have a social context; that is, it occurs within a context of social meanings which have been evolved over a long span of time. To become aware of this context is to add a new dimension of meanings to the initial activity. When the social meanings are extended to include meanings contributed by past generalizations, the activity has been provided with a historical dimension. Thus, "the true starting point of history is always some present situation with its problems."[27] In a similar manner, the immediate physical setting of an activity may derive increased meaning by its extension to a wider and wider setting. For Dewey, this widened physical setting is encompassed by the field of geography. Here too, the "starting point" of geography lies in a present, immediate activity.

History and geography as organized bodies of knowledge have only an indirect relevance to the student engaged with his subject matter. However, these organized bodies of knowledge are indispensible to the teacher; for,

> It is the business of educators to supply an environment so that this reaching out of an experience may be fruitfully rewarded and kept continuously active.[28]

Without such a store of subject matter, the teacher will be unable to lead the expanding activity in directions that will produce rewards of increased meaning.

In addition to the emerging subject matter of history and geography, science also develops use of the primary activities which constitute the subject matter of the curriculum. While the historical and geographical dimensions of an activity are simple extensions made possible by the nature of the initial activity, the development of the activity into *science* involves a qualitative change in the activity.

---

[26] *Ibid.*, p. 209.
[27] *Ibid.*, p. 214.
[28] *Ibid.*, p. 209.

It signifies conscious transfer of a meaning embedded in past experience for use in a new one. It is the very artery of intelligence, of the intentional rendering of one experience available for guidance of another . . . It aims to free an experience from all which is purely personal and strictly immediate; it aims to detach whatever it has in common with the subject-matter of other experiences, and which, being common, may be saved for *further* use.[29]

Science requires that the meanings inherent in an activity be extended to the fullest possible extent. It then requires that these meanings be formulated in the most general way. Finally, they must be ordered in such a manner as to be available for further use. Any subject matter can be "scientific" so long as it is the result of the application of scientific method or inquiry. Therefore, science in the curriculum is really the learning of the method of science in directing any activity or in dealing with any situation.

The function which science has to perform in the curriculum is that which it has performed for the race; emancipation from local and temporary incidents of experience, and the opening of intellectual vistas unobscured by the accidents of personal habit and predilection. The logical traits of abstraction, generalization, and definite formulation are all associated with this function. In emancipating an idea from the particular context in which it originated and giving it a wider reference the results of the experience of any individual are put at the disposal of all men.[30]

But what of science as organized bodies of knowledge? Where do they fit into the curriculum? How is the subject matter of science to be of direct value to the teacher? It serves as a guide in the selection of activities and in controlling their development.

Hence, what concerns him, as teacher, is the ways in which that subject may become a part of experience; what there is in the child's present that is usable with reference to it; how such elements are to be used; how his own knowledge of the subject-matter may assist in interpreting the child's needs and doings, and determine the medium in which the child should be placed in order that his growth may be properly directed. He is concerned not with the subject-matter as such, but with the subject-matter as a related factor in a total and growing experience.[31]

Thus, from Dewey's theory of inquiry there are three subject matters as such that provide the teacher with curriculum resources: history, geography, and science. These resources provide the guide for determin-

[29] *Ibid.*, p. 226.
[30] *Ibid.*, p. 230.
[31] John Dewey, *The Child and the Curriculum* (University of Chicago Press, 1902), p. 23.

ing the subject matter of the curriculum. History provides the basis for assisting the student to develop a temporal dimension to the meanings inherent in a particular activity. Geography is the basis for developing a physical dimension to the meanings of the activities. From science the method of science assists the student in organizing new meanings in the most useful way. The subject matter of the curriculum then becomes a progressive series of activities whose meanings lend themselves to a rewarding historical and physical development, and which can be usefully organized by the methods of science.

CONCLUSION

In this chapter, Dewey's theory of inquiry has been used as a basis for developing a theory of the curriculum. The nature of curriculum theory in general was shown to be determined by the basis of social inquiry itself. It will be suggestive of further inquiries and will be constantly subject to revision on the basis of subsequent inquiry. The judgments that make up the basis of curriculum theory are primarily concerned with the aims of education. Inquiry also provides a basis for determining the content of curriculum theory. From the theory of inquiry, it is possible to derive some working principles for the curriculum. Inquiry itself as an educational aim provides the principles of activity, language, and observation around which the curriculum is to be organized. Finally, the theory of inquiry contains implications for the subject matter of the curriculum. Geography, history, and science were shown as important resources for the development of the subject matter of the curriculum.

Included in this chapter were a number of difficulties that arise in connection with the conduct of social inquiries. These difficulties were suggested by Dewey himself. However, Dewey maintains that difficulties should not deter subsequent inquiry, but rather should provide an impetus to inquiry. With this in mind, in the remaining pages of this chapter one other serious difficulty connected with the relation of inquiry to the curriculum will be listed. There will also be included some encouragement as to its possible resolution.

To make abundantly clear this difficulty that arises with a secondary curriculum based upon Dewey's theory of inquiry, the responsibility of the secondary teacher will be described. At the onset, it seems a simple enough responsibility: a mere matter of devising a related series of activities. However, for these activities to have educative value, some requirements must be met. First, any activity must arouse the immediate interest of each student. Assuming this might possibly be accomplished in an elementary school where a teacher would have thirty pupils for a year and thus have an opportunity for obtaining knowledge of the interests of the pupils, such an accomplishment becomes almost impossible in the secondary school where a teacher may deal with two hundred students in a semester. But, this is not the complete story. For the very same activity must also possess intrinsic worth, engaging every student in processes that will have future value in the adult world. Nor is this all! The activity must be such as to give rise to new interests. Are the new interests to be the same for all two hundred students, or will there be two hundred different new interests, and how is such a situation to remain under the control of the teacher?

A second general requirement for the activities criterion for the teacher is that these activities must provide for intelligent growth particularly through the transition of the social function of language to its intellectual function. Here too, the expansion of meanings into larger temporal and physical dimensions must take place along with the organization of these meanings by means of scientific inquiry. This growth must be observable in all students by the teacher in order to validate the activity.

Finally, an activity must contain observable components. The activity must initiate within a situation that has directly observable features. The conclusion of an activity must also provide direct observation of the results of the activity.

The responsibility placed on the secondary teacher is overwhelming. It is little wonder that attempts to develop secondary curricula consistent with Dewey's philosophy have met with no success. However, hope should not be abandoned.

Research in the area of the behavioral sciences holds much promise for the resolution of this difficulty of the classroom implementation of Dewey's theory of inquiry. Work with programmed learning is one phase of current research. One other development that seems to give direct promise of resolving the difficult situation described above is that of the educational use of simulation being developed in many centers and universities across the country. Such uses of simulation might bear description here as a possible example of how problems should give rise to inquiries rather than despair.

Current development of simulations for educational use involves the selection of some dynamic aspects of society and incorporating these factors into the theory of games. For example, the simulation ''Napoli,'' developed by the Western Behavioral Sciences Institute of La Jolla, California, makes use of the decision-making process of legislators as the theme, where the decisions are relevant to the overall-performance of a legislative body, and which in turn determines the subsequent reelection or defeat of each legislator. Such simulations are not to be confused with role playing. Here, participants in the simulation are truly involved in an activity. As in all games, the demand is for the complete involvement of the players: one rarely plays at playing a game! To the extent that simulated factors are well integrated into game theory, so a simulation will meet the curriculum requirement of being an activity. Even more, simulations—like games—elicit the interest and require the total involvement of the student. Further, simulations are designed for varying numbers of participants, usually for 25 to 35 students, to insure a total class participation.

There are other curriculum assets that may be derived from the educational use of simulation. By the manipulation or adjustment of the mathematical model upon which the game is based, the teacher may determine in advance the general type of strategies or behavior patterns that are to meet most often with success. By means of the game, the teacher is able to reward intelligent behavior with success and more easily identify those students whose ability to think reflectively is underdeveloped.

Another asset to the curriculum from the use of simulations is that of immediacy and observation. The activity and all its elements are immediately present in the classroom. The situation and point of the game are observable factors, as is the result of each student's behavior during, as well as at the end of, the activity. The beginning, the course, and the end of the activity are readily observable to all.

The real educational ''payoff,'' however, comes from the continuing interests and high level of motivation following participation in a simulation. Researchers have labeled this phase the ''debriefing sessions.'' Here students are more anxious to extend the meanings acquired in the course of the simulation. They are anxious to compare the simulation factors with ''real life'' situations. In the case of ''Napoli,'' the debriefing raises questions such as:

(1) Is politics really the art of compromise?

(2) I voted against what I felt was right. Why?

(3) Do legislators really concern themselves only with reelection?

(4) What factors were not included in the simulation that occur in actual legislative sessions?

(5) How can the simulation be made more real?

It has been indicated briefly how simulations may provide one classroom technique that can make a Deweyian curriculum more feasible at the secondary level. A high school teacher who has been employing simulations in connection with several subject matters remarked that the day he started using simulations was the day he ceased being a *teacher* and became a *director of activities.* This is at least a step in the right direction, and it is to be hoped that continuing inquiries will further the movement.

This discussion cannot be allowed to close without mention of the similarity between a simulation and what Dewey means by a school as a "special environment." In a sense, a school as well as the curriculum is a simulation of the larger social setting in which the student will eventually find himself. The curriculum is a series of selected activities, selected because of their inherent worth. Their inherent worth is due to the fact that they have a corresponding function in society as a whole. And perhaps continuing inquiries into simulation will provide an answer to the problems that beset not only the development of curriculum theory, but social inquiry as well.

part **Three**

Language and Education

chapter 6

A View of Language

INTRODUCTION

In order to understand the perplexities that seem to arise in connection with the use of language, it is necessary to arrive at some understanding of naturally evolved language in which the difficulties are couched. Special languages, such as mathematics, are deliberately constructed, and thus any perplexities involved in special languages reflect only the limitation of the creative ability of a particular individual or individuals. On the other hand, a natural language is inherited, and the key to its understanding lies in how it functions within a society. Perplexities within a natural language cannot be understood apart from the social functioning of the language itself. Natural language is, in short, an inseparable part of man's natural history, and it functions indispensibly in man's social behavior and social development. The speaking of a language is itself an activity. As human activities increase in their variety and complexity, so do the accompanying linguistic activities. Natural languages evolve along with human societies and activities, and are equally complex. In order to come to grips with and to illuminate the complex phenomenon of language, Wittgenstein deems it desirable to "make use of certain artificial examples by means of which simple patterns of linguistic activity can be exhibited in isolation."[1] These patterns are called by Wittgenstein "language-games."

The first part of this study is concerned with the use and application of language. It constitutes a description of the view of language revealed in the *Philosophical Investigations* of Ludwig Wittgenstein.[2] This description will take place in the context of an analogy—the analogy of language-games. The variety of language-games will be noted along

[1] David Pole, *The Later Philosophy of Wittgenstein* (University of London, The Athlone Press, 1958), p. 3.

[2] Ludwig Wittgenstein, *Philosophical Investigations* (New York: The Macmillan Company, 1953), Section 23.

with consideration of the relation between language-games. By means of this analogy the linguistic processes of naming, understanding, the giving of meaning, believing, and proving will be illuminated. Also, in this part the use of language-games in the removing of puzzles and in the search for agreement will be discussed. Finally, this portion of the study will attempt to show to what extent this concept of the use and application of language is relevant to curriculum development.

Before describing and applying the analogy of language-games, it will be helpfull to say something about the general view of language taken latterly by Wittgenstein and subscribed to by many subsequent "analytic philosophers" such as John Wisdom, N. Malcolm, and O. K. Bouwsma.[3] What Wittgenstein develops is a method, that is to say, a new position from which to view language, and hence what emerges is a *view of language* rather than a philosophy of language. It is intended by Wittgenstein to be a clear view. How is it, then, that language is to be viewed? First, language is to be viewed as arising out of some specific social context or activity. What is meant here is best exemplified by considering the process by which a language is learned.

Wittgenstein's main purpose in considering how language is learned is to divest us of the notion that language is acquired through the process of naming or giving ostensive definitions. He provides an example of a primitive language:

> The language is meant to serve for communication between a builder A and an assistant B. A is building with building-stones; there are blocks, pillars, slabs and beams. B has to pass the stones, and that in the order in which A needs them. For this purpose they use a language consisting of the words "block", "pillar", "slab", "beam". A calls them out; B brings the stone which he has learned to bring at such-and-such a call. Conceive this as a complete primitive language.[4]

The knowing or learning of language involves the builder's knowing the response or reaction of a hearer to the words "block," "slab," etc. The assistant has learned the language when he has learned to perform certain actions upon hearing these words. "A child uses such primitive forms of language when it learns to talk. Here the teaching of language is not explanation, but training."[5] Hence, the learning of a language cannot be accomplished by the mere giving of names, for a name by itself tells nothing. In the initial learning of language, the verbal signs

---

[3] W. V. Quine explores a similar view in his work *Word and Object;* a work which will provide us with many useful points of comparison and illumination. Cf. Willard Van Orman Quine, *Word and Object* (Cambridge, Massachusetts: The M.I.T. Press, 1960).

[4] Wittgenstein, *Op. Cit.,* Section 2.

[5] Wittgenstein, *Op. Cit.,* Section 5.

and the activity in which they have a use are inseparable. Even in the case of ostensive definitions, to point and say ''Red!'' will mean nothing unless the individual already knows enough about the language to recognize color words as different from, say, shape words. ''Each of us learns his language from other people, through the observable mouthing of words under conspicuously intersubjective circumstances.''[6] In short, language has its source in the social activities of man. Or better, the individual's language has its source in the specific social activities in which the individual has learned its use. ''No two of us learn our language alike, nor, in a sense, does any finish learning it while he lives.[7]

To view language as arising out of and as a part of the social behavior of man will also provide some understanding of how language succeeds in communicating. For, it is the common behavior of mankind to which language can be referred and given a meaning. What both Wittgenstein and Quine are asserting here is that language has as its basis something nonlinguistic. And this nonlinguistic basis is nothing other than the social activities of mankind. Without such a basis, communication and translation become purely subjective and indeterminate. Quine points out that communication does take place, and most uniformly in connection with activities that matter socially. So, even though ''no two of us learn our language alike,''

> Different persons growing up in the same language are like different bushes trimmed and trained to take the shape of identical elephants. The anatomical details of twigs and branches will fulfill the elephantine form differently from bush to bush, but the overall outward results are alike.[8]

Again, viewing language as a social activity, it is recognized that language is without an essence. In other words, there is no single feature common to all activities in which language plays a role. The employment of language in connection with activity A may involve characteristics 1, 2, and 4. And activity B may involve characteristics 3, 4, and 5, while a third activity, C, may be identified by characteristics 3, 5, and 6. Thus, while there are shared features between activities A, B, and C, there is no feature common to A and C. Language, then, is a generic term covering a wide range of activities whose use or definition cannot be given by a single set of necessary and sufficient characteristics or *essences*. For example, the definition of a triangle as ''a plane surface bounded by three straight sides'' may be said to contain the essence of triangularity. ''A plane surface bounded on three sides'' provides the

[6] Quine, *Op. Cit.*, p. 1.
[7] *Ibid.*, p. 13.
[8] *Ibid.*, p. 8.

necessary and sufficient conditions for all triangular objects to be identified and correctly called *triangle*. This will also exclude all nontriangles. Few words, however, can be defined in such an *essential* way; language is not one of them. If language is without an essence, then there can be nothing compelling about the use of words or grammar. There can be no basis for some universal objective standard of correctness in the use of words or in the forming of sentences. The notion of a single model for language must be rejected. But how is the existing uniformity among, say, speakers of English to be explained?

> The uniformity that unites us in communication and belief is a uniformity of resultant patterns overlying a chaotic subjective diversity of connections between words and experience. Uniformity comes where it matters socially; hence rather in point of intersubjectively conspicuous circumstances of utterance than in point of privately conspicuous ones.[9]

The final point to be noted in connection with Wittgenstein's view of language is that there is nothing concealed in language. Much misunderstanding concerning the nature of language comes from the tendency to want to think about language rather than to look at language to see how it actually functions. Wittgenstein's view of language is not going to teach anything new about language, but really, "we want to *understand* something that is already in plain view. For *this* is what we seem in some sense not to understand."[10] Or again, Wittgenstein suggests that our problem concerning language will most likely be solved by "looking into the workings of our language, and that in such a way as to make us recognize those workings: *in despite of an* urge to misunderstand them."[11] Quine also warns against the mistaken notion that there is a "sub-basement" to our language, a place where hidden meanings, hidden understanding may lie.

> There is every reason to inquire into the sensory or stimulatory background of ordinary talk of physical things. The mistake comes only in seeking an implicit sub-basement of conceptualization, or of language. Conceptualization on any considerable scale is inseparable from language, and our ordinary language of physical things is about as basic as language gets.[12]

The importance of this last aspect of Wittgenstein's view of language will become more evident later in this study when the notions of meaning, understanding, proving, and so forth are examined. For it is the notion that there is something hidden in language or beneath language

---

[9] *Ibid.*, p. 8.
[10] Wittgenstein, *Op. Cit.*, Section 89.
[11] *Ibid.*, Section 109.
[12] Quine, *Op. Cit.*, p. 3.

that has led to many misconceptions about language and into what Wittgenstein terms "philosophical perplexities."

To recapitulate, Wittgenstein encourages a fresh look at language. First, Wittgenstein has admonished his readers to look at how a language is learned, and when this is done, it is found that language is a matter of training rather than of naming or the giving of definitions. Next, when Wittgenstein investigates how language communicates, he finds that it communicates by virtue of the fact that it has its life in the behavioral patterns of mankind, and it is to this objective behavior that language refers and from which language takes its meaning. Another point to which Wittgenstein draws attention is that language is essentially without an essence. By this Wittgenstein wishes to note that there is no common characteristic of language as a whole, but rather there are as many different languages as there are types of behavior in which language has a part. The notion that the use of a sign is inseparable from the sign itself is another important part of this view of language, for the sign itself is nothing apart from the role it plays in a particular social activity. Finally, Wittgenstein insists that there is nothing hidden in language; that what is required is merely to look at the objective role it plays in human behavior and the nature of language will be clear, and many of the perplexities that arise from the use of language will disappear or be clarified. In short, then :

> What seems to emerge from all this is that speaking a language, which, of course includes understanding things said in it, is a matter of being able to *do* a variety of things, to act or behave in certain ways— and to do so under the appropriate conditions. Some of these skills are purely linguistic: a person unable to construct grammatically correct English sentences could not be said to speak English. But others are nonlinguistic—or, rather, are at once linguistic and nonlinguistic—in that they involve an interaction between using words and behaving in nonlinguistic ways.[13]

There is one further point that might be noted in connection with Wittgenstein's view of language. From the previous points it becomes clear that in a general sense ordinary language, that is, natural language, perfectly suffices for most everyday needs. The problem of language then, it would appear, originates in the attempt to use ordinary language in context or in connection with activities for which language or the particular language being used was not originally intended. Wittgenstein, of course, is particularly interested in this in connection with philosophy and philosophical problems.

---

[13] George Pitcher, *The Philosophy of Wittgenstein* (Englewood Cliffs, New Jersey: Prentice Hall, Inc., 1964), p. 242.

Ordinary language was not designed with the philosopher's special interest in mind; its purpose is to allow human beings to communicate with one another so that work can be accomplished, transactions can be carried out, wishes can be expressed and satisfied, and so on. And for these purposes, ordinary language is quite adequate.[14]

LANGUAGE-GAMES

The notion of language-games is meant to be taken as an analogy. The purpose of this analogy is basically therapeutic; that is, it is designed to cure "mental cramps." Wittgenstein maintains that what is held is most often a wrong picture of language. First of all, there exists a tendency to see language as a unity or as something that possesses an essence, and too much time is lost in seeking this essence or those factors which are common to all words. There is also the wrong notion that there is basically something wrong with ordinary language. That is, ordinary language is basically inadequate to fully express the various meanings, understandings, feelings, mental pictures, and so forth. This is to say that there is something hidden or concealed beneath or within words, the words themselves being mere separate entities and the real meaning lying somewhere behind. Now the purpose of this analogy or the way in which it will help cure mental cramps is to exchange the previous picture of language as a unity possessing an essence and that something is basically wrong with ordinary language, for a picture that will be perhaps less misleading. Or, as Wittgenstein says, "my aim is: to teach you to pass from a piece of disguised nonsense to something that is patent nonsense."[15] Wittgenstein would like his analogy of language-games to encompass this entire range of language activities. In short, he wishes the "whole, consisting of language and the actions into which it is woven," to be called the language-game."[16]

In order to understand the applicability of this analogy of language-games, the analysis of the notion of "game" will be required. This will reveal how various ways in which the use of the word game corresponds to what has been previously said concerning Wittgenstein's view of language in general. Begin first with the notion of the essence of *game*. If the use of the word game is examined carefully, is there found in its use an essential unity? Consider the variety of games, and ask whether or not there is an element which is common to all. Consider the games of football and baseball. Surely there are certain elements here that both games possess in common. But on the other hand, consider the game of

[14] *Ibid.*, p. 226.
[15] Wittgenstein, *Op. Cit.*, Section 464.
[16] *Ibid.*, Section 7.

football with the game of chess. What is there here in common? Or, the game of solitaire with the game of hopscotch. What is really found here is what Wittgenstein would call "a family resemblance," but nothing that can be called an essential common element. In short, the term game refers to a variety of activities, all of which may be said to bear a resemblance, and certain ones may have elements in common, but the range of the spectrum is a broad one so that the common element between games such as football and chess disappears.

> Consider for example the proceedings that we call 'games.' I mean board-games, card games, ballgames, Olympic games, and so on. What is common to them all?—Don't say: 'There *must* be something in common, or they would not be called games'—but *look and see* whether there is anything in common to all.—For if you look at them you will not see something that is common to *all*, but similarities, relationships, and a whole series of them at that. To repeat: don't think, but look![17]

How is it, then, that games are learned? First of all, it is seldom that a game is learned by sitting down and memorizing a list of rules of the game. It can be generally seen that in the vast majority of cases a game or the rules of the game are learned along with the activity itself and as a part of the activity. And in still other cases, a game is learned simply by imitating the behavior of others. In short, the learning of a game does not mean the mere knowledge of the rules, but rather the ability to participate in an activity in which the rules serve as a limiting factor for the activity.

The question may now be asked, "What is hidden in a game?" This is the same question that was put in connection with language. What is meant here is that in viewing the social activity of a game is there anything such as a hidden motive present? It might be inquired as to whether there would be a game at all if both opponents in a game were not aware of the point of the game, or would the game have any meaning to a spectator who did not know what the point of the game was. Hence, everything that would be meant by the word game is obvious in the activity itself. There can be no hidden motive of a baseball manager in a particular move for his motive is obvious: to win the game and to win it within the context of the rules of which the players, coach, and spectators are aware.

Again, it may be inquired as to whether or not the rules of a game are not in a sense something separate and apart from the game itself. Do they coexist? Upon examination, it would appear that a set of rules in themselves would have little, if any, meaning unless the point of a game

---

[17] *Ibid.,* Section 66.

and the kinds of activities and circumstances under which these rules were to apply were already understood. Hence, the rules and the point of the game are not to be thought of as something separate and distinct from the game itself, but rather both rules and point are to be thought of as different phases of the same type of social behavior.

It should be noted, then, that there are a number of points of comparison that may be drawn between the notion of game and Wittgenstein's view of language, enough to warrant the use of the analogy of games as a means of further illuminating the role of language. It must be kept in mind, however, that this is indeed an analogy; there is no intention here to imply that language is a game, but rather that if language is treated as if it were a game, then many pitfalls that currently perplex the individual in the study of language may be avoided. This point will be further illustrated in the following pages when the application of the analogy to various problems and concepts within language itself will be investigated, such as the concepts of naming, believing, understanding, and so forth. It is these important applications of the analogy of language-games that must be described next.

NAMING

The first point that emerges from the consideration of the act of naming as illuminated by the analogy of language-games, is that naming is not the process by which a language is learned. Consider, for example, what it is to learn a name. Consider the child when he first parrots a word; it will be observed that this is not what is ordinarily expected of a person learning a name; rather it is more akin to simply making a mark or a sound. A parrot could do as well, or an idiot. What is more usually meant by a child "learning" a word is that he has learned to respond in certain ways upon hearing, seeing, or uttering the word. For example, a child's first utterance of "daddy" is accepted as a sign of advancement in language only if accompanied with the proper overt behavior indicating association with the child's father rather than, say, with the family pet. The making of a sound or a mark is not a sufficient condition for saying that one has *learned* a language. On closer scrutiny, it will be found that language is actually used in giving and learning names. For example, to ask, "What is the name of this?" presupposes the ability to use language. "When we say: 'Every word in the language signifies something' we have so far said *nothing whatever;* unless we have explained exactly *what* distinction we wish to make."[18]

---

[18] *Ibid.,* Section 13.

Another important point that emerges when the activity of naming is closely scrutinized is that naming does not involve a single relationship or a single activity. Philosophers have expended a great deal of time and energy seeking for the relationship that links the name with the things named, but such an activity reflects in Wittgenstein's view nothing more than man's natural craving for unity. Actually, the whole problem of this relationship between the name, marks on a paper, and the thing designated is resolved by simply putting the name back into the context, the activity in which it has played a role. In the language-game cited previously in this chapter, in which a builder called to an assistant the names "slab," "block," and so forth, what the word slab designated here is nothing more than the elicitation of the response of having this object brought by the assistant to the builder. Yet, in other contexts, or rather in other games, the word slab will certainly have some other relation to the object it designates.

> Perhaps the best way to express Wittgenstein's position would be as follows. In a trivial sense of 'name' and 'denote,' all, or at least most, words name or denote something. This, however, says very little. The word 'name,' like the word 'game,' covers a multitude of different cases: there is no one essential name-relation, any more than there is a single essence common to all games. There is a certain relation (or groups of relations) between the name 'John Jones' and the man John Jones, and a different one (or group) between the word 'red' and red things—but if you think that for every word, and in particular for 'meaning' and 'understanding,' there exists things to which they bear just *those* kinds of relations, then you are sadly mistaken.[19]

In the previous paragraphs the functions of naming have been described. It is now necessary to see how Wittgenstein treats the notion of a name itself. Wittgenstein shows the relationship between a name and its role in language-games or in a game itself by using as an example the game of chess.[20] And just what does it mean in a game of chess to name a piece? The name of a piece in a game of chess certainly does not tell anything about the use of, say, the pawn. Also it would seem that knowing the name pawn does not assist, or rather is not essential, in the learning of the rules of a game. In fact, it would be quite possible to learn the rules of the game of chess without ever having seen a chessman. In what sense, then, does the giving of a name such as in the statement "This is a pawn." have any meaning at all? The name pawn will have meaning or reveal to a learner of chess the use of this piece in the game only if in a sense "the place is already prepared." What Wittgenstein is trying to convey here is that in order for the word pawn to be

---

[19] Pitcher, *Op. Cit.*, p. 277.
[20] Wittgenstein, *Op. Cit.*, Section 31.

anything more than a mere sound or marks on a piece of paper, the hearer must already know something of the game of chess or in some cases even be ''master of a technique.'' As a matter of fact, the individual learner of the game of chess must already know what is meant by ''a piece in the game'' and other things as well, before a name can tell him anything.

Naming itself, then, ought to be thought of as a number of related language-games, the name itself being considered as merely a piece in the game and by no means the whole game. Hence, each language-game consists of pieces or names of its own, and the act of naming itself is, in fact, a variety of language-games.

> That is really to say: we are brought up, trained to ask: 'What is that called?'—upon which the name is given. And there is also a language-game of inventing a name for something, and hence of saying, 'This is . . .' and then using a new name.[21]

In bringing this section to a conclusion, it should be noted that naming is not to be considered as a primary source of language. It is true that in some trivial sense the ability to use names or to learn or to acquire names is certainly a basis of language, but in any nontrivial sense it will be found that those names which have any significance must be learned in connection with an activity or within a behavior pattern. A name by itself is nothing. It is only when its use and the rules of the game in which this name is to play a part are understood, that the name takes on meaning and significance. It is in this sense that Wittgenstein suggests that names be considered as analogous to pieces in a game. He further suggests that the act of naming itself, or the giving of names, be viewed as constituting a language-game, or better, a series of related language-games in and of themselves. Such a view of the act of naming provides relief from the necessity of seeking for some mysterious relationship between a name and the thing named.

> It will suffice to recall Wittgenstein's recommendation to seek, not for objects corresponding to words and sentences, but for their function in human life as parts of language.[22]

MEANING

Turning now to an application of the analogy of language-games to the notion of meaning, a broad distinction must be made. This is the distinction between meaning as denoting one specific thing in terms of

---

[21] *Ibid.*, Section 27.
[22] Pole, *Op. Cit.*, p. 16.

language activities, and meaning as possessing certain common factors independent of the activities in which the term may occur. To rephrase this in terms of the analogy, the following questions will be posed. Is there only one language-game in which we employ *meaning?* Does *meaning* occurring in various language-games exhibit a common factor or essence? In as much as the second question presupposes a negative response to the first, these questions are not meant as a basis of inquiry, but rather as a means of presenting Wittgenstein's thoughts on meaning. Each of these questions will now be considered in turn.

Is there only one language-game in which we employ *meaning?* This question is asking, in brief, for the meaning of meaning. Before the question can be asked as to the meaning of the word, an understanding of what is required by the way of an answer must be arrived at.

> 'The meaning of a word is what is explained by the explanation of the meaning.' Ie: if you want to understand the use of the word 'meaning,' look for what are called 'explanations of meaning.'[23]

Looking, instead of analyzing the meaning of meaning, it will be found that the meaning of a word (including *meaning*) as well as the sense of a sentence consists in its use. For example, what is being asked for when it is inquired, "What is the meaning of the character of Ophelia in Hamlet?" Or, "What does sigma mean in mathematics?" Or, "What is the meaning of the current crises in Africa?" Or, "Do you really mean it?" Or, "Did you mean Sam Johnson or Ben Jonson?"

> And so it is with the word 'meaning.' It is fruitless to take it out of all context and ask 'What does meaning mean?' or 'What is the meaning of a word?' These questions only reinforce the illusion that the meaning of a word is a mysterious entity of some sort. We must consider the term 'meaning' more concretely: Wittgenstein urges us to think not of what meaning is all by itself, but of what it is to explain the meaning of a word to teach the meaning of a word to a child. (Similarly, not 'What is time?' but 'What is it to measure time?'; not 'What is a statement?' but 'What is involved in making a statement?')[24]

Hence, Wittgenstein rejects the notion that meaning constitutes a role in a particular language-game or even that meaning constitutes by itself a unique language-game. Rather, Wittgenstein urges that meaning

---

[23] Wittgenstein, *Op. Cit.*, Section 560.

[24] Pitcher, *Op. Cit.*, p. 250.

Note: Quine makes a similar observation when he says "A liklier place to seek the cause is in the difference between how we, whose mother tongue is English, learn 'bachelor' and how we learn 'Indian nickel.' We learn 'bachelor' by learning appropriate associations of words with words, and 'Indian nickel' by learning directly to associate the term with sample objects." See Quine, *Op. Cit.* p. 56.

be viewed as having a role to play in a variety of language-games, and the particular role has no significance apart from the particular game in which it is employed.

Now the second question arises, ''Does meaning, occurring in various language-games, have an essence? One possibility that occurs is that somehow *meaning something* refers to some sort of mental act; that is, something goes on in the speaker's mind as he utters a word or phrase. And, it is this something that bridges the gap between words as mere sounds and the objects to which they refer. It gives meaning to the sounds.

In assuming that meaning can be equated with something like mental acts, it is possible to be led to certain absurdities. For example, if it were claimed that these mental acts are the same as a mental image or picture in an individual's mind, then this claim would very quickly lead into an infinite regression. If the meaning of ''red'' is derived from the picturing of a certain red spot in the mind, then from what source or what basis is the selection of that particular red spot as the basis for the meaning of ''red'' made? As a matter of fact, the existence of a picture or a mental image of redness in no way affects the individual's ability to use the word red or of any hearer to correctly interpret this meaning. The word has meaning with or without the accompanying mental picture. For as Wittgenstein says:

> If I say 'I meant *him*' very likely a picture comes to my mind, perhaps of how I looked at him, etc.; but the picture is only like an illustration to a story. From it alone it would mostly be impossible to conclude anything at all; only when one knows the story does one know the significance of the picture.[25]

Still, an individual may maintain that what he intends by a mental act is not so much a picture but rather a sort of pointing out. This is to say that something analogous to pointing out an object with a finger goes on in the mind when the individual means some particular thing. For example, when an individual says, ''That is brown,'' he is meaning the color of the object rather than its size or shape or the material of which it is made. It can be suggested that when such a statement is made the individual is focusing his attention upon the color of the object. However, as in the case of mental pictures, this act of concentration or act of pointing out fails to do that which it is supposed to do. Or perhaps it is better said that language accomplishes the task it is intended to do whether or not the mental act of pointing out in fact occurs. In short, such an act neither adds nor detracts from the ability of the word to function in the language.

[25] Wittgenstein, *Op. Cit.*, Section 663.

The point is that when meaning is spoken of as a kind of mental activity, attention is focused on the wrong thing. Such "wrong headedness" encourages the individual to look into his own head or mental activities for the source of meaning rather than looking around him for the source of meaning that springs from linguistic activities themselves.

> "When I teach someone the formation of the series . . . I surely mean him to write . . . at the hundredth place."—Quite right; you mean it. And evidently without necessarily even thinking of it. This shows you how different the grammar of the verb 'to mean' is from that of 'to think.' And nothing is more wrong-headed than calling meaning a mental activity! Unless, that is, one is setting out to produce confusion. (It would also be possible to speak of an activity of butter when it rises in price, and if no problems are produced by this it is harmless.)[26]

Wittgenstein also rejects the notion that meaning can in any way be equated with the thing denoted. The meaning of a name is not the object it denotes. The difficulty in maintaining this view can be seen at once from the following example. When Mr. N dies, it is correct to say that the bearer of the name N dies. Moreover, if the name N really does lose its meaning when its bearer, Mr. N, goes out of existence (which would be the case if the meaning of the name were the object it denotes), then it made no sense to say "Mr. N no longer exists," or "Mr. N is dead." But of course it makes perfectly good sense to say these things.[27]

> It is important to note that the word 'meaning' is being used illicitly if it is used to signify the thing that 'corresponds' to the word. That is, to confound the meaning of a name with the bearer of the name.[28]

Now, another language-game in which meaning has a role is that of language analysis itself. Is it not true that the business of analysis is to make meanings clear and precise? Wittgenstein rejects this notion. For to suggest that there can be a standard of exactness apart from the context in which a word is used is at best misleading. It makes little sense to ask for an analysis of the word time in such a way as to make this notion more exact or more precise. How precise does a wrist watch have to be in order to serve the function for which it is intended? And yet this same standard of exactness would not work at all in a physics laboratory, while the request to "be on time for dinner" requires a still different measure of exactness. Hence, no analysis of time can be based or have as its purpose the establishment of a standard of exactness

---

[26] *Ibid.*, Section 693.
[27] This example is taken from Pitcher, *Op. Cit.*, p. 181.
[28] Wittgenstein, *Op. Cit.*, Section 40.

established independently from the context in which it is being considered.

It must be considered, then, that "meaning" as it occurs in various language-games does not have an essence or common factor. "The variety of ways in which words acquire their meanings is reflected in the variety of their uses."[29]

UNDERSTANDING

Wittgenstein's treatment of understanding is quite similar to his treatment of meaning. He stresses that understanding has no essence, that is, there is no factor common to all situations in which the word understanding is used. A good deal of time is spent by Wittgenstein in analyzing what for him is our most common misconception of the notion of understanding, that is, when the word understanding is used what is being referred to is some sort of mental process or processes. In the case of meaning the concern was with bridging the gap between the word and the person who hears or responds to the word. Now, for Wittgenstein certain mental processes may indeed justify our saying, "I understand," but no such process can be shown to be identical with what is meant by understanding. Wittgenstein wants to show how misleading it is to consider the word understanding as a description of a mental state. "One might rather call [it] a 'signal'; and we judge whether it was rightly employed by what he goes on to do."[30] Finally, as Wittgenstein examines the various language-games in which understanding plays a role, it becomes evident that the only criterion or test of understanding which could be said to be applicable in all situations is the actual success in application. For a clarification of these points, it will be useful to fall back on one of Wittgenstein's major examples:

> Let us imagine the following example: A writes a series of numbers down; B watches him and tries to find a law for the sequence of numbers. If he succeeds he exclaims: 'Now I can go on!'—So this capacity, this understanding, is something that makes its appearance in a moment. So let us try and see what it is that makes its appearance here.—A has written down the numbers 1, 5, 11, 19, 29; at this point B says he knows how to go on. What happened here? Various things may have happened; for example, while A was only putting one number after another, B was occupied with trying various algebraic formulae on the numbers which had been written down. After A had written the number 19, B tried the formula $a_n = n^2 + n - 1$; and the next number confirmed his hypothesis.[31]

[29] Pole, *Op. Cit.*, p. 14.
[30] Wittgenstein, *Op. Cit.*, Section 180.
[31] *Ibid.*, Section 151.

But this is not the only possible accounting of what has gone on when B has exclaimed "Now I can go on!" Possibly he asks himself: "What is the series of differences?" He discovers 4, 6, 8, 10 to be the differences and he says, "Now I can go on." Or possibly the series is one with which he is already well familiar and hence only needs to recognize this, and then simply responds, "Now I can go on." Thus, if his understanding a series, that is, being able to assert: "Now I can go on," is to be described as a mental process, then it is clear that it is not a single mental process, for there are many processes that can be going on and each in turn can justify his saying: "Now I can go on." But the question still remains to be answered, "Does understanding really mean just these mental processes, either the one or a combination of them?" Is it not possible that it can be mistakenly said, "Now I can go on"? And, if it is a mistake, that is, if it is found that the individual is unable to complete the series, does it make sense to say, "I did understand but now I don't"? In brief, Wittgenstein wishes to have it clearly understood that our confusion arises from our attempt to think of understanding as a mental process. The mental processes which may or may not accompany understanding are at best a justification for uttering such a statement as: "Now I can go on." But the real test of understanding seems to lie in the individual's capacity to, in fact, go on, that is, complete the process. In an analogous sense the same applies to understanding a command. The real test of understanding a command lies in the ability to carry it out as intended by the person giving the command. And surely there are commands to which an individual may respond without any mental process going on whatsoever: an automatic response. "Knowing how to go on" is not the only common equivalence that can be attached to the verb *to understand*. Wittgenstein asks that the grammar of the verbs *to fit* and *to be able* be considered. He suggests the consideration of the following exercises:

> (1) When is a cylinder C said to fit into a hollow cylinder H? Only while C is stuck into H? (2) Sometimes we say that C ceased to fit into H at such-and-such a time. What criteria are used in such a case for its having happened at that time? (3) What does one regard as criteria for a body's having changed its weight at a particular time if it was not actually on the balance at that time? (4) Yesterday I knew the poem by heart; today I no longer know it. In what kind of case does it make sense to ask: 'When did I stop knowing it?' (5) Someone asks me 'Can you lift this weight?' I answered 'Yes.' Now he says 'do it!'—and I can't. In what kind of circumstances would it count as a justification to say 'When I answered "yes" I *could* do it, only now I can't'? The criteria we accept for 'fitting,' 'being able to,' 'understanding,' are much more complicated than might appear at first sight.[32]

[32] *Ibid.*, Section 182.

In conclusion, it should be noted that Wittgenstein is giving a notion of what *understanding* essentially isn't. That is to say, Wittgenstein is showing how understanding is not essentially a mental process. There isn't any criterion that can be uniformly applied to all instances of understanding apart from the success of the behavior resulting from such understanding.

> Would it be correct to say that it is a matter of induction, and that I am as certain that I shall be able to continue the series, as I am that this book will drop on the ground when I let it go; and that I should be no less astonished if I suddenly and for no obvious reason got stuck working out the series, than I should be if the book remained hanging in the air instead of falling?—to that I will reply that we don't need any grounds for *this* certainty either. What could justify the certainty *better* than success?[33]

Now if Wittgenstein is concerned with demonstrating what understanding isn't, does he have anything to say concerning what understanding is? It can certainly be inferred that if understanding is without an essence, then one is severely handicapped in attempting to give a precise definition of the term. Hence, it may be concluded that for Wittgenstein the question of what understanding is becomes unanswerable apart from a particular language-game in which it occurs. The perplexities that arise when a common meaning of understanding is sought are dissolved when the activity or language-game in which this term has a role to play is observed.

BELIEVING AND PROVING

In dealing with notions of believing and proving, Wittgenstein again urges that they be viewed from the context (language-game) in which they actually occur. Such a view will quickly dissolve the notion that believing and proving have essences, that is, a common factor present in all cases of their use. Also, the notion that the meaning of such concepts are essentially limited to some sort of mental activity will be dissolved.

Consider by way of example the notion of *proving*. One way of considering proving is to inquire as to how an assertion is justified. And where is such a justification to be sought? The language-game must first be noted. Justification of an assertion concerning the weather might require the behavior pattern of going outdoors and looking—but also, perhaps, looking at barometers, wind gauges, and so forth. The specific game in which weather assertions are couched will determine what will be accepted by way of justification, whether the assertion is made as a

---

[33] *Ibid.*, Section 324.

passing neighborly comment or in a serious meteorological discussion. ''Inference'' is often spoken of as justifying assertions.

> But don't I infer that a chair is there from impressions, from sense data?—I make no inference!—and yet I sometimes do. I see a photograph for example, and say 'There must have been a chair over there' or again 'From what I can see here I infer that there is a chair over there.' That is an inference; but not one belonging to logic. An inference is a transition to an assertion; and so also to the behavior that corresponds to the assertion. 'I draw the consequences' not only in words, but also in action.[34]

An example of the notion of *believing* must now be considered. Wittgenstein poses the question of whether a thought can be an ''expression'' of belief (hope, expectation, and so forth). '' 'In spite of everything that he did, I held fast to the belief . . .' Here there is thought, and perhaps a constant struggle to renew an attitude.''[35] ''But believing is not thinking. (A grammatical remark.)'' ''The concepts of believing, expecting, hoping are less distantly related to one another than they are to the concept of thinking.''[36]

> Ask yourself: What does it mean to *believe* Goldbach's theorem? What does this belief consist in? In a feeling of certainty as we state, hear, or think the theorem? (That would not interest us.) And what are the characteristics of this feeling? Why, I don't even know how far the feeling may be caused by the proposition itself.

> Am I to say that the belief is a particular colouring of our thoughts? Where does this idea come from? Well, there is a tone of belief, as of doubt.

> I should like to ask: how does the belief connect with this proposition? Let us look and see what are the consequences of this belief, where it takes us. 'It makes me search for a proof of the proposition.'—Very well; and now let us look and see what your searching really consists in. Then we shall know what belief in the proposition amounts to.[37]

It might be interesting to note at this point that Quine in his section on ''evidence''[38] expounds a similar view. Quine maintains, along with Wittgenstein, that words have meaning only in the sentences in which they occur, and that the criteria of their meaning lies in the resulting behavior. ''Any realistic theory of evidence,'' says Quine, ''must be inseparable from the psychology of stimulus and response, applied to sentences.''[39] Now it might seem that under such conditions the notion of

---

[34] *Ibid.*, Section 486.
[35] *Ibid.*, Section 575.
[36] *Ibid.*, Section 574.
[37] *Ibid.*, Section 578.
[38] Quine, *Op. Cit.*, p. 17.
[39] *Ibid.*

evidence or of proof might be extremely difficult to establish; after all, each individual has developed his own unique and complex system of conditioning. However, insofar as there are common behavior patterns among individuals, there will be "points of general congruence." It is these points that provide a basis for agreement. These "points of general congruence" can be identified with what Wittgenstein would call family resemblances among language-games. It might be noted at this point that there is an area in which Quine and Wittgenstein do not appear to be in perfect accord. This is on the notion of simplicity. While Wittgenstein feels that one of the severe restrictions to our understanding of language lies in the insistence upon seeking for essences (unity in language), Quine feels that this seeking for unity and simplicity is an essential part of the quest for knowledge. In fact, Quine goes on to say:

> Whatever simplicity is, it is no casual hobby . . . The neurological mechanism of the drive for simplicity is undoubtedly fundamental though unknown, and its survival value overwhelming.[40]

Nevertheless, there seems to be no discord between Wittgenstein and Quine, or at least there is no inconsistency in attributing Quine's view on scientific method and truth to what Wittgenstein might have said had he spoken on the subject.

> Have we now so far lowered our sights as to settle for a relativistic doctrine of truth—rating the statements of each theory as true for that theory, and brooking no higher criticism? Not so. The saving consideration is that we continue to take seriously our own particular aggregate science, our own particular world theory or loose total fabric of quasi-theories, whatever it may be. Unlike Descartes, we own and use our beliefs of the moment, even in the midst of philosophizing, until by what is vaguely called scientific method we change them here and there for the better. Within our own total evolving doctrine, we can judge truth as earnestly and absolutely as can be; subject to correction, but that goes without saying.[41]

LANGUAGE-GAMES AND THE REMOVAL OF PUZZLES

It will be recalled that Wittgenstein's main concern and the main point of his work was a removal of philosophical puzzles. His concern was with philosophy; however, it does not seem essential to assume that his analogy of language-games must be limited in its application to puzzles that are essentially philosophical. If Wittgenstein's view of language is accepted (the view of language as essentially being an activity or one central type of social behavior), it would seem to follow that whenever puzzles or perplexities of any type are confronted, the first

---

[40] *Ibid.*, p. 20.
[41] *Ibid.*, pp. 24-25.

requirement or step that should be taken for their removal is to determine whether or not the source of these puzzles lies in the language itself. How is the determination to be made as to whether or not the source of perplexities lies in language or in some objective condition or set of conditions? It is to the development of such a method that Wittgenstein's philosophical investigations are devoted. What Wittgenstein is suggesting is that the way in which language is used be viewed in a different manner from that in which it is customarily looked at. If from this different point of view the perplexities and puzzles remain, then there is at least some evidence that the source may be in an objective condition rather than in language itself. On the other hand, if an individual is confronted with a puzzle and will take the time to ask himself what language-game is being played, he may find that by identifying the particular social activity in which the words involved in the puzzle are actually used, that the puzzle itself will disappear.

Wittgenstein describes his method in respect to philosophical problems in this way:

> We must do away with all *explanation*, and description alone must take its place. And this description gets its light, that is to say its purpose—from the philosophical problems. These are, of course, not empirical problems; they are solved, rather, by looking into the workings of our language, and that in such a way as to make us recognize those workings; *in despite of* an urge to misunderstand them. The problems are solved, not by giving new information, but by arranging what we have always known. Philosophy is the battle against the bewitchment of our intelligence by means of language.[42]

Puzzles, then, particularly puzzles of the philosophical rather than the empirical type, may be solved (if not dissolved) from gaining this "clear view of language."

> A main source of our failure to understand is that we do not *command a clear view* of the use of our words.—Our grammar is lacking in this sort of perspicuity.[43]

To repeat, then the formula by which puzzles of a nonempirical nature may be solved is to seek the language-game in which the words that are the source of the puzzle have a role to play, and hence, a meaning.

LANGUAGE-GAMES AND THE SEARCH FOR AGREEMENT

Not only is there interest in the removal of a puzzle, but often mankind occupies itself with a search for agreement. It will be of interest to note how the notion of language-games can play a part or at least

[42] Wittgenstein, *Op. Cit.*, Section 109.
[43] *Ibid.*, Section 122.

account for, if not aid in, this search. David Pole, critically commenting on Wittgenstein's work, makes the point that: "The essence of rational discourse is the search for agreement. Wittgenstein's failure to take account of it, I suggest, prejudices his whole picture of language."[44] This, it should be suggested, is an unfair comment. It was mentioned previously in this paper that there was a divergence of emphasis between Wittgenstein and Quine on the search for simplicity, unity, or, if it may be added, agreement. But where Quine is talking about simplicity, he is referring to human motivation—to the social activities of men as the primary source of language. Then, it would seem that the entire point of Wittgenstein's work is that the notion of unity, the notion of the search for agreement or simplicity, has gotten out of hand insofar as it has been applied to language. This, in fact, is one of the primary sources of the puzzles and perplexities that arise within the context of language itself. The point of David Pole's criticism is that ignoring man's search for agreement, man is being condemned to a permanent maintenance of *status quo*. In fact, Pole would say that if there is no possibility of agreement on the linguistic level there can be no progress, no change in man's social conditions. But Wittgenstein would say:

> 'So you are saying that human agreement decides what is true and what is false?'—It is what human beings *say* that is true and false; and they agree in the *language* they use. That is not agreement in opinions but in form of life.[45]

Hence, it would seem that Wittgenstein would maintain that where significant change occurs, it occurs in the behavior of man, in his social activities. New language-games do not come into existence independently, but they come into existence or grow into existence out of a particular social activity. What Wittgenstein shows is that an agreement at the linguistic level is of little importance or consequence unless it is reflected in or derived from social behavior. It would seem that Mr. Pole's objection stems from a wrong view of language.

Still, what does this method contribute to man's search for agreement? The answer to this question may be summarized in the following way. In identifying the source of disagreement, it must first be determined that no matters of fact or additional information can settle the dispute in favor of one participant or the other. It must also be determined that the nature of the dispute is not logical, that is, that no matter of logical ruling can settle the question at stake. Once these two notions have been removed, then it will be possible to move to the second phase of reaching agreement. The possibility of reaching agreement on this

[44] Pole, *Op. Cit.*, p. 59.
[45] Wittgenstein, *Op. Cit.*, Section 241.

verbal level now depends on the ability to demonstrate the context or the language-game in which the words of the dispute have meaning.

In other words, what is given here is a demonstration to clearly indicate the type of language-game in which the terms of a dispute not only have meaning but which would lead or provide a disposition to answer "yes" or to assent to the issue of dispute. But this is not sufficient. It is also necessary to indicate those language-games in which there would be the disposition to respond in the negative and in which the terms of the dispute also had a role or meaning. In short, once the possible uses of the terms of the dispute have been laid out and the decision has been reached as to which of these uses would provide a basis for assent and which for dissent, the possibilities for agreement have then been exhausted. Such a description by no means guarantees that an agreement will be reached, but it simply exhausts the possible basis on which hope for agreement may rest. To the extent that disagreement lies in the misuse of language, the above procedure should provide the basis for agreement. However, if the disagreement lies in other sources, then this procedure should also make that fact abundantly clear.

chapter 7

From Language-Games
to Education

INTRODUCTION

In the preceding chapter, Wittgenstein's approach to language was briefly described. The analogy of language-games was developed as a device that captured the main features of Wittgenstein's view of language as well as providing a convenient means of applying this view to specific areas of language. The function of the analogy of language-games in Wittgenstein's overall philosophy is to provide a mental picture of language that will correct the "wrong-headed" view that creates "mental cramps" or perplexities. The analogy of language-games is by no means an incidental part of Wittgenstein's philosophy, but represents the central theme.

> We come now to the aspect of using words that plays by far the most important part in Wittgenstein's later philosophy—namely, their use in what I have called speech activities . . .
>
> Wittgenstein's name for what I have called a speech activity is "language game!"[1]

It would seem advisable at this point to reiterate and reemphasize two main points concerning the analogy of language-games. First, it should be kept in mind that the analogy of language-games was intended to be applied as a method, particularly a method for the solution or dissolution of problems arising from a misuse or from a wrong view of language itself. Such problems are, of course, most commonly observed in the field of philosophy. Second, the analogy of language-games is based upon a particular view of language. It is a view that includes language among the other social activities of mankind. Language becomes in this view just another facet of man's social behavior. Language

---

[1] Pitcher, *Op. Cit.*, p. 239.

activities, like games, are distinguished by the variety of activities that are associated with them, and, like games, language has its points and its rules. However, the relationship between language-games is best described as a family resemblance.

Also, it should be clearly understood at the outset of this chapter that Wittgenstein himself made no reference to education, the processes of education, or in particular to curriculum or schooling. His interest was in the solution of philosophic problems. This, of course, gives rise to the question regarding the extent to which Wittgenstein's method for the solution of problems and his view of language are relevant to education. It would appear that the only answer necessary to this particular study would be to the effect that Wittgenstein's method and views of language are relevant to education to the extent that language itself is relevant. The organization, administration, and development of institutions of education, including discussions and decisions based upon aims, goals, and theories of education, can be pointed to, and it can be noted to what extent language plays a role therein. Also, to consider the process of teaching itself is to recognize that language would appear to be in some degree relevant. Philosophers of education with such divergent views as Jacques Maritain and John Dewey acknowledge an important role for this symbolic process in the educational enterprise itself. For the purpose of this chapter, then, it will be necessary to assume that language does indeed have some relevance to education. However, the degree of relevance will be left to the reader and his own particular views of education.

Assuming some degree of relevance, then, it will be useful to demonstrate specifically what kind and how extensive a theory of curriculum can be generated from Wittgenstein's analogy of language-games and the methods and view of language inherent therein. It is hoped that a demonstration can produce a more relevant basis for deciding the value of Wittgenstein's work to the enterprise of education in general and to curriculum in particular.

Wittgenstein's analogy of language-games may be usefully applied in the development of a curriculum theory in two major areas. First, it may be usefully applied as a method of clarification of issues, postulates, and assumptions from which a curriculum theory is to be developed. Second, the analogy of language-games can be useful in providing a method for organizing the curriculum itself. In other words, the sort of curriculum theory derivable from Wittgenstein's analogy of language-games will have two aspects: first, a procedure for clarification; and second, this procedure applied to language will be seen to produce a basis or rationale for the organization of the curriculum itself. Each of these two areas will be considered in turn.

LANGUAGE-GAMES AND CURRICULUM CONSTRUCTION

The task here will be to examine the analogy of language-games as a method for the clarification of curriculum problems. That is to say, an examination will be made of how the analogy of language-games might be used to clarify some of the concepts, aims, and purposes often associated with the problems of curriculum development. The concepts used will be those which Wittgenstein had occasion to deal with; this in order to insure more accurate employment of the method. However, it is not intended that the method be limited necessarily to these concepts.

As the first example, Wittgenstein's treatment of the notion of meaning will be considered. The word meaning is often encountered in conversations, discussions, and in works dealing with curriculum theory and in particular with criticisms leveled against the curriculum itself. For example, the title of a current work by Philip Phenix, *Realms of Meaning*,[2] indicates the author's central theme and chief proposal concerning curriculum revision. Also, in a recent article, Joseph J. Schwab inquires into the "Structures of the Disciplines: Meanings and Significances."[3] There are numerous varieties of "everyday statements" concerning meaning: "What do you *mean* by self-realization?" "Our children are not being taught the *meaning* of democracy!" "Our children are learning words but not their *meanings!*" As was indicated in the earlier discussion, when the analogy of language-games is applied to the notion of meaning it becomes evident that there are two senses in which meaning can be most generally analyzed. First, the notion of meaning is used to inquire for the specific meaning of words themselves. Also, an inquiry into the meaning of "meaning" may be made. That is, what is being asked for when the meaning of anything is asked for? For example, when a child is required to know the meaning of the word democracy, the analogy of the language-game would first of all direct attention to the particular use or role in the game that the word democracy is playing. Is democracy here referring to a set of social institutions, political institutions, an economic system, individual behavior patterns, and so forth? It will be seen that the term democracy has quite a distinct and different use in each of these settings or games. And, until there is a clear notion of the particular game, there can be no clear notion as to the meaning of the word in this particular case. Hence, keeping the analogy of language-games in mind will assist in the laying down of the

[2] Philip H. Phenix, *Realms of Meaning* (New York: McGraw-Hill Book Company, 1964).

[3] Joseph J. Schwab, "Structures of the Disciplines: Meanings and Significances," in *Structure of Knowledge and the Curriculum*, G. W. Ford and L. Pugno, eds. (Chicago: Rand McNally & Company, 1964), p. 1ff.

basis for curriculum theory by serving as a reminder to continually ask for the particular context, the particular game, and the use within the game of a particular word or concept about which there is a concern.

An apt illustration of the problem of meaning will be provided after a second way in which the analogy of language-games aids in clarifying the issue is described. The request concerning meaning is made clear when it is noted that the term meaning itself does not possess an essence. This is to say that the meaning of "meaning" itself is dependent upon the particular game or context in which it arises. For instance, if there is concern with a child's knowing the meaning of democracy, the meaning of science, the meaning of discipline, and so forth, what is really being demanded of the child? If the analogy of language-games is kept in mind, one thing certainly will be clear: the same thing is not required in each case. Therefore, it will be incumbent upon those designing a curriculum or laying down a plan for curriculum development to specify the precise requirements or criteria by which it shall be determined whether or not a child has acquired the meaning of democracy, of science, of discipline, and so forth. In some instances, having or acquiring meaning may consist merely in the ability to repeat a formal definition, or to give some other type of linguistic response. On the other hand, meaning or the having of meaning may require as a condition for its verification some manifestation of overt behavior. For example, it is most usual to expect commands to have meaning only in connection with a particular circumstance. If I am lying on the beach and call to someone to "Close the door," it may be said in one sense that the words "close the door" have a meaning; but, in a situation marked by the absence of any door or any need to close one were it present, this command loses what is normally thought of as its meaning. Hence, to ask for the meaning of words is to ask for the conditions under which they are to be used. And the word meaning itself is without meaning unless we specify clearly the conditions of its use.

An excellent example of the perplexities that may arise in connection with meaning is provided by Philip Phenix's work, *Realms of Meaning*.[4] In this work Phenix develops the notion of "realms of meaning" upon which he then constructs a theory of the curriculum. What are the conditions of the use of meaning in this work? What for Phenix is the meaning of "meaning"?

In an early chapter, Phenix cites G. E. Moore, Bertrand Russell, and Ludwig Wittgenstein as inspirational thinkers.[5] He then concludes:

---

[4] Phenix, *Op. Cit.*
[5] *Ibid.*, p. 40.

This recent philosophical emphasis on distinct logical orders of meaning and on the clarification of human understanding by the analysis of the actual uses of symbols is basic to the philosophy of curriculum set forth in these pages. While the method of treatment used herein is not predominately that of the language analysts, the present work presupposes a similar commitment to the exposition of meanings-in-use and parallel conclusions as to the multiple patterns of human significa- tion.[6]

If such an analysis is "basic" to Phenix's views, then may it not be assumed that so key a term as meaning will be understood by its actual uses? When Phenix asserts that "there is no single quality that may be designated as the one essence of meaning,"[7] it would appear that this is to be the case. Further statements also indicate an agreement with the views of Wittgenstein.

> By 'working understanding' is meant the ability to use sounds (or visual symbols), concepts, and grammatical devices in accordance with the accepted customs of the particular language community.[8]

On the other hand, some perplexity begins to arise when the reader encounters such statements as "the six realms . . . provide the founda- tions for all the meanings that enter into human experience."[9] Wittgen- stein's views would seem to stand in direct opposition to such a state- ment. Wittgenstein makes every effort to show how meanings *grow out of* human experience and activities. In no sense could his analysis even suggest that meanings exist apart from the activities out of which they have grown. Phenix further indicates that "the fragmentation of experi- ence . . . is one of the sources of meaninglessness."[10] "Fragmentation" would not imply for Wittgenstein the loss of meaning or "meaningless- ness." Rather, any loss of meaning would be the result of the failure to acknowledge the fragmentation. It is the attempt to impose a unity upon activities where there is none that renders symbols meaningless. The perplexity is further increased when Phenix suggests that the "various kinds of meaning" have an "intrinsic logical order."[11] That meaning has any intrinsic features would be inconsistent with Wittgenstein's posi- tion. Any "order" that might be possessed by some "kinds of meaning" is derived from the order within the activity itself.

At this point it is appropriate to try to determine what the meaning of "meaning" is for Phenix. It was previously noted that for Phenix, in seeming accord with Wittgenstein, there is no "one essence of meaning."

---

[6] *Ibid.*, p. 41.
[7] *Ibid.*, p. 5.
[8] *Ibid.*, p. 69.
[9] *Ibid.*, p. 8.
[10] *Ibid.*, p. 9.
[11] *Ibid.*, p. 9.

Does this indicate that for Phenix meaning has no essence? This is, of course, Wittgenstein's position. Meanings for Phenix may be of different kinds, but that each has an ''intrinsic logical order'' would seem to indicate an essence. Meaning, it would appear then, has for Phenix a *sort of* essence. A look into the way language is to be learned might further delineate the differences between the two positions.

> The test of a person's knowledge of a language is whether or not he can use it. Though he may be able to speak words and recite grammatical rules, if he cannot actually organize the words into intelligible discourse, he does not really understand the language. The language is a form of human behavior, and language teaching is a mode of modifying human behavior. The sovereign rule in teaching is to demonstrate language in use and to develop correct habits of speech by reinforcing desirable speech behavior.[12]

This seems clear enough and in accord with Wittgenstein's view on the subject. However, on the following page an assertion is found to the effect that language ''is not a skill to be learned as one would master a manual technique.''[13] Compare this with Wittgenstein's statement: ''To understand a language means to be master of a technique.''[14] Here perplexity again takes over! But, another clue to Phenix's meaning of ''meaning'' appears.

> What is now becoming clear is that meanings depend on structure rather than structures on meaning, and therefore that meaning is best served by concentrating attention on grammatical structure.[15]

Now a *picture* of meaning begins to emerge: meaning has an essence. This essence is the logical structure of language. Logical structure precedes meaning, and meaning precedes the use of language. Logical structure is intellectually, not behaviorally, derived. Such a picture of language would appear to be the very ''wrong-headed'' one that Wittgenstein wished to ''cure us of.''

The notion of understanding is also one that continually crops up in discussions of curriculum and curriculum development. How does Johnny come to *understand* what he learns? Do the students really *understand* science? Do the students really *understand* democratic processes? Here it would appear that individuals concerned with the curriculum and schooling are not just asking whether or not meaning is being provided, but really, something more is being asked for. What is this something more? Here again the analogy of language-games can be of assistance. As indicated in the previous chapter, the analogy of

[12] *Ibid.*, p. 62.
[13] *Ibid.*, p. 63.
[14] Wittgenstein, *Op. Cit.*, Section 199.
[15] Phenix, *Op. Cit.*, p. 67.

language-games leads to the rejection of the notion that understanding has an essence, or rather that it has a common usage in language. Hence, if there is to be any coming to grips with the notion of understanding, some other criterion must be looked to than mental activity, namely, to behavior itself. But again, behavior in general cannot be looked to, but rather the specific behavior relevant to that context in which understanding is desired. When the curriculum developer wishes to create a situation for the promotion of basic understanding, the analogy of language-games prompts the immediate inquiry: "Understanding of what?" In other words, in what specific circumstances or in what specific activity or game is it desired that understanding take place? Then, it must further be inquired: given this particular activity in which understanding is desired, what criteria of behavior will justify the assertion that now the individual understands? Wittgenstein provides one specific answer to the question of what is required in understanding and that is "knowing how to go on." In short, one criterion for the establishment of understanding is the ability of an individual engaged in an activity to continue that activity independently. However, each activity carries with it its own set of criteria for the determination of understanding. And such criteria must be based not on some mental activity but on some form of behavioral activity, either linguistic or nonlinguistic.

Another concept that can use some clarifying in connection with the development of curriculum theory is the notion of proving or providing evidence for those statements that are made concerning the aims and purposes of education. And here again, the analogy of language-games directs our attention to the specifics of the case. For it is also found here that the criteria for the necessary and/or sufficient conditions of proof in one situation will not be adequate for some other situation, for example, the different kind of evidence required to confirm the statement that "The time of the eclipse on Sunday will be . . ." And compare the evidence required to confirm the statement that "The time of Sunday dinner will be . . ." Questions concerning the verification of the fundamental statements of curriculum construction can be resolved by posing two questions. First, what are the sufficient conditions (or condition) that would cause an individual to accept as true the particular statement in question? Second, what are the conditions (or condition) under which the same individual would reject as false the statement under consideration? This method of referring to a specific game or games under which certain propositions are true or false can certainly serve to establish whether or not basic agreements on fundamental propositions are matters of linguistics or whether they rest in some other fundamental dispositions. This means of reaching agreement is one all too frequently overlooked in matters of educational theory.

Suppose, for example, that a school board is confronted with the proposition that sex education should be included in the high school curriculum. And the proof of this proposition cannot be established to the satisfaction of all board members by the appeal to some *a priori* standard. A suggested procedure consistent with the view of language here presented will be to have each board member list a set of conditions under which he will accept the proposition as true and acceptable. Also, he will list a set of conditions under which he will consider the proposition false and, hence, unacceptable. Armed with these lists, the superintendent can then determine whether or not a *proof* of the proposition can be constructed so as to make it acceptable to all board members, or whether or not there existed some fundamental attitudes of a contradictory nature such as to preclude any general argument as to the validity of the proposition by all board members. The question that the superintendent must pose to himself is: "Is there a single situation or state of affairs toward which all board members will feel disposed to assent to 'sex education'?" If there is such a situation, then he can hope for full board approval of the initial proposition.

Finally, it should be noted that the analogy of language-games is designed to cure the tendency to seek panaceas in dealing with any major social problem. Certainly, this is as true in the field of education as in any other. The analogy of language-games tends to focus attention on specific problems rather than to seek for essences or common factors among whole groups of problems. Here again, there seems to be an area in which the analogy of language-games can provide a real service. Prior to drawing up a set of general prescriptions for the development of curriculum, it should be required that first the thinking on specific issues be clarified and that the problems of the curriculum be dealt with one by one.

THE ANALOGY OF LANGUAGE-GAMES AS A METHOD OF CURRICULUM ORGANIZATION

When the view of language reflected in the analogy of language-games is applied, it is possible to identify certain criteria for the organization of the curriculum. This is based, of course, upon certain assumptions and conditions: the assumption that language is a relevant factor in the education of children, and the recognition that to fully demonstrate the scope of such a factor it will be necessary that it be considered the sole factor.

The first and foremost statement that can be made in connection with the organization of the curriculum is simply that the curriculum should be organized in terms of language-games. The particular kinds of linguistic activities that are to be included in the curriculum must be identified, and such activities are to be included first and foremost as discreet and separate activities. The difficulties of this simple sounding task will be described shortly. First, however, family resemblances must be considered.

Even though each language activity is discreet and in a sense unique, there are indeed family resemblances among the various activities or games. For example, Wittgenstein suggests that language-games run the gamut from such activities as praying and swearing to that of forming and testing a hypothesis. However, while the forming and testing of a hypothesis in physics certainly bears a resemblance to the forming and testing of a hypothesis in history, the two are by no means identical. Still they bear a closer resemblance to each other than either of them bear to the forming and telling of a story.

It would seem that while the decision as to what should be included in the curriculum ought to be based upon particular language activities or particular language-games, it does not appear to be inconsistent to suggest that once this decision is made, the language-games themselves might be grouped into those games which bear a family resemblance. Again, by means of an example, the language-games arising from man's political activities may bear certain resemblances to each other; also, man's social activities give rise to another set of language-games which may not be totally distinct from each other. Man's approach to his physical environment again gives rise to a set of language-games which bear a marked resemblance to one another. However, the point in so grouping language-games into families is to put the student in a position of noting the subtle differences between the particular games rather than the family resemblances. Such a grouping would also clearly emphasize the fact that it is due to the striving for economy that many uses are provided for the same term, but at the same time clearly illustrating that because the same term is used in many activities it does not necessarily follow that it retains one meaning throughout. Such a grouping would train students to inquire as to the particular point and rules of the specific game in order to discover the meaning of the terms used therein.

Also, the organization of the curriculum by language-games and into families of games provides a double check upon the understanding derived by the students. First, the understanding of a student might be checked by his ability to effectively engage in a specific language-game. A second check upon the student's understanding would be by determining his ability to effectively engage in a family of games—to pass from one to another without confusion or perplexity. Hence, while learning a specific activity, the students would at the same time be developing that subtle understanding and awareness of the various uses of language itself.

There are, as suggested earlier, a number of difficulties associated with the determination of which language-games would be appropriate to the secondary curriculum. These difficulties are by no means insurmountable but would require a great deal of painstaking research and analysis. To illustrate some of the difficulties, a relatively simple example may be taken; consider the usual high school subject of physics. Suppose that it were deemed desirable to insure that all high school graduates understood physics. What language-game or games would be engaged in by the high school students?

Initially, it must be made clear what physics is not. Physics cannot be considered as a formal body of knowledge. A formal body of knowledge is rather the *result* of a language activity or activities. Also, the notion that physics constitutes a single language-game must be rejected. The divergent fields of quantum mechanics, relativity mechanics, and elementary particle physics need only be considered to illustrate this point.

Physics is, in fact, made up of a large number of language-games. If the topic of light alone is considered, then how many distinct activities might be identified as primarily language activities? Such distinct language activities can be identified in connection with determinations of the quantity of light, its quality, its effect, its sources, and its transmission. But, in stating these language-games in this fashion they are seen to be characteristic of the language-games engaged in by physicists. Thus, physics may be analyzed into a large number of language-games —the language-games of physicists.

A more serious problem arises when it is asked whether or not the language-games of physicists are the best kind of activities for bringing students to an understanding of, say, the effect of light. Perhaps a language-game centering on art could develop the same meanings in a more effective way. It may be possible and desirable for graduate students in physics to imitate the language activities of physicists, but it does not follow that it is either possible or desirable for high school students to do so. Further analysis and inquiry would be necessary even to discern fully the scope of this problem.

A similar problem exists concerning the grouping of language-games into categories of family resemblances. It can be recognized that there might be some strange bedfellows. Learning to use the word light in physics would involve language-games in which quantity, quality, effect, sources, and transmission of light played a role. Those language-games or activities could range from activities in art, photography, chemistry, biology, botany, and so forth. Yet, among all these and others there would be a family resemblance—all would be contributing to the use of light. All would be activities in which light plays a role.

Therefore, for society to indicate that physics is to be understood by high school students provides very little help to the educator. What particular ideas or physical concepts are to be understood? Into what language-game or games are they to be translated? On what basis or on what priority are family resemblances to be determined? Are language-games when grouped by family resemblances best presented to the students as grouped in time? These and other questions are more easily asked than answered. It can be anticipated that a curriculum theory implemented by answers to these questions and problems would involve the student in activities far different from those currently associated with secondary schools.

From the organization of the curriculum around language-games and groups of language-games, another asset accrues. Matters of agreement and disagreement, especially on issues involving value judgments, are often viewed as semantic issues. Thus, the issue lends itself to easy solution: a matter of defining disputed terms. However, if such acts do not lead to agreement, it is then agreed to disagree. Thus the solution becomes purely relative—a matter of personal preference or taste. By grouping studies in terms of language-games it can soon be seen that agreements are not merely reached on a linguistic level, but rather are matters of agreement in a form of life or of a particular kind of social activity. In short, agreements or disagreements are not merely as to how to use words, but rather on the nature of the game itself and the points and rules of the game; these rules and points reflect a particular social activity, a particular way of life. Therefore, agreement here is more than merely a linguistic matter.

It should be noted here that such an organization also indicates certain procedures or pedigogical approaches that would be required of teachers themselves. Clearly, the primary task of the teacher would be to teach a form of linguistic behavior. Each teacher would be a teacher of language, not language in general, but a particular language and the particular activity from which such language arises. The question, of course, might be raised: if all teachers are teaching a form of linguistic behavior, what then of the language teacher? Obviously, the language teacher would not become obsolete. The English language itself, for example, has a family resemblance with all those activities in which English is spoken. This resemblance lies in what Wittgenstein calls surface grammar. And indeed, this would be sufficient content for teachers of English.

A final word may be said with reference to the contribution of language-games to the development of a curriculum theory. It is that such an approach to curriculum theory provides the developer of the theory with a means of objective evaluation of the theory itself. For the evaluation would be based upon the subsequent linguistic behavior of those who had been subjected to this curriculum, or possibly to their development of the desired linguistic behavior. This desired linguistic behavior (from what has been previously laid down as mere outline) would consist in the student's approach to the determination of a meaning, the test that he would apply to determine understanding, the method he would employ in reaching an agreement, and whether or not the student would be willing to deal with problems on an individual basis and resist the temptation to solve a variety of problems with a single solution.

To summarize briefly by way of conclusion to this chapter, first, it has been indicated how Wittgenstein's notion of language-games and the view of language from which it was derived can be used to provide a procedure or method for the clarification of some of the aims and purposes of the curriculum. Such a procedure can also be of great assistance in reaching an agreement on matters of purposes and aims of the curriculum. There has been no intention either to suggest that Wittgenstein offers any prescription concerning the fundamental issues in curriculum development, or has it been intended to derive from his view any such prescriptions. It has also been indicated that the analogy of language-games does indeed provide a basis for the organizing of a curriculum. The prescription or assumption that must be made in this connection is simply that language or language activities are to some extent relevant to the education of youth. However, there is no prescription made in connection with which language-games should be included or excluded from the curriculum. Of course, the grouping of the language-games in the curriculum into those which bear family resemblances will be dependent upon the determination of what language-games will be included. Clearly, then, it would be impossible to make more specific recommendations regarding the curriculum either in its fundamental aspects or in its organization. This can emerge only after such matters as the purposes and aims of the curriculum have been decided upon.

chapter 8

Conclusion

In the preceding chapters, certain statements were drawn from three philosophical notions or concepts. These three sets of statements were meant to provide to the fullest possible extent three guides for the development of curriculum theories consistent with the particular concepts. In so doing, the educational relevance of these three concepts was illuminated. More indirectly, the relevance to education of the general philosophic positions from which these concepts were drawn was illustrated. There remains to be asked in this final chapter whether or not there are any conclusions to be drawn from the curriculum theories derived from three seemingly disparate philosophical positions.

The following pages will describe three general conclusions that appear warranted by the three previously described curriculum theories. They are as follows:

(1) The notion of "discipline" or fixed subject matter as the basis for curriculum construction will be rejected.

(2) The generic term analysis may be used to describe the fundamental aim or concern of the secondary curriculum.

(3) The basis for evaluating the content of the curriculum will be the resulting behavior of the students.

The second and third general conclusion may be taken as constituting a general curriculum theory consistent with all three philosophical positions. Some additional research needed to implement such a curriculum theory will be suggested.

The concluding portion of this chapter will present a brief argument based upon the relevance of contemporary philosophies to formal education and *deducing two social imperatives* for the schools.

THE REJECTION OF FIXED SUBJECT MATTER

Much contemporary writing on the secondary school curriculum seems to constitute an attempt to find new or more modern means of justifying the *academic disciplines* as the basis and content of the curriculum. Such attempts are typified in the works of such individuals as Philip Phenix, Joseph Schwab, and the joint work of Arthur King and John Brownell.[1] All these writings basically seek to use the activities and the results of the activities of mathematicians, physicists, historians, and other "scholarly" professions as the model for the secondary curriculum and as a primary aim of public education. There is also the implication in these works that the more fundamental disciplines are somehow permanent and enduring; hence, the secondary curriculum need vary little over considerable periods of time. The three contemporary philosophical concepts of language-games, inquiry, and freedom described in the present work imply secondary curriculum theories totally inconsistent with the notion of a fixed subject matter and/or academic disciplines as the basis and content of a curriculum.

In Chapter 7 of this work, the application of Wittgenstein's analogy of language-games was used as a basis for developing a theory of the secondary curriculum. The resulting theory revealed that the secondary curriculum was to be organized around language-games, that is, around specific linguistic activities. It was shown that such disciplines as physics do not in themselves constitute a single language-game, but rather a whole set of related linguistic activities. Further, it was indicated that the activities of physicists are not necessarily the best language activities for developing initial understandings of physical concepts. Physics, as a body of knowledge, is the *result* of a number of related language-games; it is not a linguistic activity. The varied activities in which physicists engage are constantly undergoing change, often changing at such a rate that the family resemblances among the linguistic activities of physicists are frequently temporarily lost. The kinds of language activities or language-games appropriate to promoting an understanding of some physical concept are also subject to constant modifications and changes, and can never be fully exhausted. Recall the example of *light* cited in Chapter 7. How many language activities are there in which the word light has a use, a meaning? Does "understanding the concept of light" require that light be correctly used in the language-game at hand, or does it require that the individual be able to correctly

---

[1] Philip Phenix, *Op. Cit.;* Joseph Schwab, *Op. Cit.;* Arthur R. King, Jr. and John A. Brownell, *The Curriculum and the Disciplines of Knowledge* (New York: John Wiley & Sons, Inc., 1966).

use the term in all language-games where it plays a role? If it is the latter case, then little if any understanding exists in the world! Thus, the language activities or games to be included in the secondary curriculum pose a difficult problem, one not solved by a selection from among academic disciplines. The solution to this problem cannot result in any fixed content of the curriculum, as no curriculum could include all language-games relevant to understanding a single concept, not to mention the variety of concepts implicit in most aims of education.

It is equally clear that from the curriculum theory derivable from Dewey's theory of inquiry no fixed subject matter can form the secondary curriculum. For Dewey, the organized bodies of knowledge or disciplines are themselves constantly undergoing inquiry and hence change. Even allowing for such change, however, subject matter conceived of as organized bodies of knowledge is inadmissible as the content or subject matter of the curriculum. Subject matter as the content of the curriculum is for Dewey composed of student activities or students engaged in activities. The activities must meet certain criteria laid down by Dewey. One such criterion is that of student interest. This criterion alone precludes the fixity of subject matter, for students' interests seldom remain constant from year to year. The opposition of Dewey to a fixed subject matter is well known and need not be belabored here.

The curriculum theory derived from Sartre's concept of absolute freedom also stands opposed to any notion of a fixed subject matter as curriculum content. Consistent with the individual's freedom is the position that all knowledge is intuitive. Knowledge intuited by the individual is in the strict sense "his knowledge." It is appropriated by means of his free act—by his freedom. The individual is free only "in situation," that is, free only in relation to his particular situation. Thus, any implication of an external structure imposed from without upon knowledge or the curriculum presupposes an essence of human nature and of knowledge. Such an implication is contrary to human reality which is freedom. To include any such structuring within the curriculum places the school in the position of directing the youth toward an unauthentic life and encouraging acts of bad faith.

ANALYSIS

Having briefly indicated one common agreement between the three described curriculum theories as being what a basis or content of a curriculum theory is *not*, something must now be said about the common positive elements. The first of these has been labeled "analysis." This term may prove an unfortunate choice on the part of the present writer; however, it will be hastily added that analysis is intended as a generic term, one encompassing three sorts of activities. That these three activities share something in common will be made clear, but that what they share is properly called analysis is merely suggested—being a topic that would carry far beyond the limits of the present work.

Wittgenstein's analogy of language-games is meant to provide an aid for the analysis of ordinary language. When this analogy is applied to a specific linguistic activity, it enables the individual to see a word as deriving its meaning from the specific context in which it occurs. In short, this activity of ordinary language analysis is composed of taking a troublesome word from the context in which the trouble arises and placing this word in a concrete setting in which the word has a definite use or role. By so doing, the troublesome word has been placed in a setting where its use, and hence meaning, is clear for all to see.

Dewey's theory of inquiry provides a description of the successful analysis of problems. Training in inquiry is training in the ability to see a problematic situation in terms or in a frame of reference that will be suggestive of operations for bringing about a solution. A totally indeterminate situation is insoluble. It must be placed in the context of a problem, which involves determining certain facets of the situation in such a manner as to provide fruitful suggestions to possible means of solution. The first step of inquiry, then, is to picture an indeterminate situation in a new partially determinate context—the context of a problematic situation. Further analysis of the problematic situation produces suggested operations for a solution of the situation which is confirmed or rejected on the basis of specific observations of the results of the operations when applied to the situation.

Man's absolute freedom, according to Sartre, is manifest only in situation. It is only through the analysis of self that the individual's situation is revealed to him along with his freedom. The analysis of self reveals to the individual his freedom: that is, it reveals that the individual is totally the result of his free choices made in relation to his "facticity," and thus he creates himself in situation. Free choices are not a matter of wistful thinking, but rather they involve a commitment to action. An individual's choices are revealed to himself and others through his actions. From an existential point of view, what is analyzed by the individual are his actions. They are analyzed in such a way as to reveal to the individual his choice of projects and of self. Existential analysis, then, would seem to consist primarily in the individual viewing his acts in such a way that they reveal to him his essential freedom and the contingency of the world and values. It is the placing of the individual's acts in the context of absolute freedom. Success of the analysis is revealed in the moral or authentic quality of subsequent acts.

EVALUATION IN BEHAVIORAL TERMS

The second positive element found to be common in the three derived curriculum theories is that of the method or criterion of evaluation. It is here being suggested that not only does analysis itself begin with and involve behavior, but that the criterion for the evaluation of analysis lies also in patterns of behavior. For example, consider Wittgenstein's language-games. To understand the meaning of a word is to be able to use this word correctly in a language activity in which the word plays a role. For a child to be said to know certain words, the mouthing of such words is not a sufficient criterion; rather, the child must accompany the mouthing with appropriate forms of behavior. This is what Wittgenstein meant when he said, "If a lion could talk, we could not understand him."[2]

In Dewey's views, the behavioral basis for evaluation is equally emphasized. The problematic situation is resolved when the tensions between an individual and his environment from which the situation emerged are eliminated, allowing the individual to resume his "normal course." Furthermore, the resolution of a problematic situation is itself observable, for the problematic situation will have undergone a change.

The only criterion provided by the existentialism of Sartre for the determination of whether or not the individual has fully analyzed his situation is that of the quality of his actions. A person cannot correctly analyze his situation without accepting his absolute freedom. Therefore, the quality of an "escape from freedom" or bad faith will be absent from his actions. The individual will assume himself as "being his acts" and will accept full responsibility for them and himself.

CONCLUSION

From a consideration of the three curriculum theories presented in this work there have been drawn three common elements. If these elements could be considered as a basis of a joint curriculum theory, the situation might be summed up as follows. First, this curriculum theory would exclude any attempt to establish a fixed, formal subject matter as the basis for curriculum content. Second, the curriculum content or subject matter would be primarily constituted by the activities engaged in by the students. More specifically, the activities would focus upon one or more of the three forms of analysis: (1) the analysis of language, (2) the analysis of problematic situations, and (3) the analysis of the human situation and self. Third, the various activities of the curriculum would

---

[2] Wittgenstein, *Op. Cit.*, p. 223e.

be constantly evaluated by reference to the developing or changing behavior patterns of the students.

Such a curriculum theory, while appearing simple as to statement, would by no means constitute a simple job to implement. Consider, for example, the fact that little or no work has been done in determining how the various forms of analysis here presented can be adapted to the various levels of student maturity. Further, there is no work available indicating specific kinds of behavior patterns to be used as standards of expectancy at various stages of education. For example, what kind of behavior patterns might reasonably be expected at the eighth grade level to indicate authenticity, problem solving ability, and language analysis? In fact, the suggestion of analysis as the basis for a curriculum theory opens a wide area for new inquiries rather than providing any real solution to curriculum problems.

On the other hand, if the suggestion that the three common elements might be considered as a curriculum theory is rejected, the following may be considered. If philosophy or the philosophic enterprise represents an analysis of the standards, goals, and values of a society, if schools are viewed as social institutions whose primary function is to prepare the youth for active participation in the society, and if it may be allowed that the three philosophical positions discussed here represent a cross section of contemporary philosophy, then it must be concluded that the schools should give more emphasis to the activity of analysis in its various forms than is currently the case. Also, teachers should be better trained to observe and evaluate student behavior patterns as indications of the results of the curriculum—and not merely test behavior.

Bibliography

Alberes, R. M., *Jean-Paul Sartre: Philosopher Without Faith,* translated by Wade Baskin, The Wisdom Library, a division of Philosophical Library, New York, 1961.

Alston, William P., *Philosophy of Language,* Foundations of Philosophy Series, Prentice-Hall, Inc., Englewood Cliffs, New Jersey, 1964.

Archambault, Reginal D., ed., *John Dewey on Education,* selected writings, The Modern Library, New York, 1964.

Barnes, Hazel E., *Humanistic Existentialism,* University of Nebraska Press, Lincoln, 1938.

Barrett, William, *Irrational Man,* Doubleday Anchor Books, Doubleday and Co., Inc., Garden City, New York, 1958.

Blackham, H. J., *Six Existentialist Thinkers,* Harper and Row Publishers, New York, 1952.

Bouwsma, O. K., "The Blue Book," *Journal of Philosophy,* Volume LVIII, No. 6, 1961.

Burke, Kenneth, *Linguistic Approach to Problems of Education,* Part 1, The Fifty-Fourth Yearbook of the National Society for the Study of Education, *Modern Philosophies and Education,* University of Chicago Press, Chicago, Illinois, 1955, pp. 259-303.

Chappel, V. C., ed., *Ordinary Language,* Contemporary Perspectives in Philosophy Series, Prentice-Hall, Inc., Englewood Cliffs, New Jersey, 1964.

Cumming, Robert Denoon, ed., *The Philosophy of Jean-Paul Sartre,* Random House, New York, 1965.

Desan, Wilfrid, *The Tragic Finale,* Harper Torchbooks, Harper and Brothers, New York, 1954.

Dewey, John, *Art as Experience*, Capricorn Books, G. P. Putnam's Sons, New York, 1934.

———, *The Child and the Curriculum*, Phoenix Books, The University of Chicago Press, 1902.

———, *Democracy and Education*, The Macmillan Company, New York, 1916.

———, *Essays in Experimental Logic*, Dover Publications, Inc., New York, 1916.

———, *Experience and Education*, Collier Books, New York, 1938.

———, *How We Think*, D. C. Heath and Company, Boston, 1933.

———, *Knowing and the Known*, with A. F. Bentley, Beacon Press, Beacon Hill, Boston, 1949.

———, *Logic, The Theory of Inquiry*, Holt, Rinehart and Winston, New York, 1938.

———, *Philosophy and Civilization*, Capricorn Books, New York, 1931.

———, *Philosophy of Education, Littlefield*, Adams & Company, Paterson, New Jersey, 1946.

———, *The Quest for Certainty*, G. P. Putnam's Sons, New York, 1929.

———, *Reconstruction in Philosophy*, The Beacon Press, Boston, 1920.

Flew, Antony, ed., *Logic and Language* (first and second series), Anchor Books, Doubleday and Co., Inc., Garden City, New Jersey, 1951; 1953.

Ford, G. W., and Lawrence Pugno, *The Structure of Knowledge and the Curriculum*, Rand McNally and Co., Chicago, 1964.

Frank, Philipp, *Philosophy of Science*, Prentice-Hall, Inc., Englewood Cliffs, New Jersey, 1957.

Geiger, George R., *John Dewey in Perspective*, McGraw-Hill Book Company, New York, 1958.

Greene, Norman N., *Jean-Paul Sartre, The Existentialist Ethic*, The University of Michigan Press, 1960.

Grene, Marjorie, *Introduction to Existentialism*, The University of Chicago Press, 1948.

Hardie, Charles Dunn, "The Philosophy of Education in a New Key," in *Educational Theory*, October, 1960, reprinted in Joe Park, ed.,

Selected Readings in Philosophy of Education, Macmillan Co., New York, 1958 and 1963.

Harper, Ralph, "Significance of Existence and Recognition for Education," in *Modern Philosophies of Education,* The Fifty-Fourth Yearbook of the National Society for the Study of Education, Part 1, Nelson B. Henry, ed., University of Chicago Press, Chicago, 1955, p. 215ff.

Hartnack, Justus, *Wittgenstein and Modern Philosophy,* translated by Maurice Cranston, Anchor Books, Doubleday and Co., Inc., Garden City, New York, 1962.

Heinemann, F. H., *Existentialism and the Modern Predicament,* Harper Torchbooks, Harper and Row, New York, 1953.

Kaufmann, Walter, *Existentialism from Dostoevsky to Sartre,* Meridian Books, New York, 1957.

King, Arthur R., Jr., and John A. Brownell, *The Curriculum and the Disciplines of Knowledge,* John Wiley and Sons, New York, 1966.

Kneller, George F., *Existentialism and Education,* Philosophical Library Inc., New York, 1958.

Mayer, Frederick, *New Perspectives for Education,* Public Affairs Press, Washington, D. C., 1962.

Molina, Fernando, *Existentialism as Philosophy,* Prentice-Hall, Inc., Englewood Cliffs, New Jersey, 1962.

Morris, Van Cleve, "An Overview: Existentialism and Education," reprinted in Joe Park, *Selected Readings in the Philosophy of Education,* The Macmillan Co., New York, 1958, p. 535ff.

Murdoch, Iris, *Sartre: Romantic Rationalist,* Yale University Press, New Haven, 1953.

Newsome, George L., Jr., "Analytic Philosophy and Theory of Education," in *Proceedings: Philosophy of Education Society,* June, 1960, reprinted in Joe Park, *Selected Readings in Philosophy of Education,* The Macmillan Co., New York, 1958 and 1963.

Olson, Robert G., *An Introduction to Existentialism,* Dover Publications, Inc., New York, 1962.

Phenix, Philip H., *Realms of Meaning,* McGraw-Hill Book Co., New York, 1964.

Pitcher, George, *The Philosophy of Wittgenstein,* Prentice-Hall, Englewood Cliffs, New Jersey, 1964.

Pole, David, *The Later Philosophy of Wittgenstein*, University of London, The Athlone Press, 1958.

Quine, Willard Van Orman, *Word and Object*, The M.I.T. Press, Cambridge, Massachusetts, 1960.

Ratner, Joseph, *Intelligence in the Modern World*, The Modern Library, Random House, New York, 1939.

Reichenbach, Hans, *The Rise of Scientific Philosophy*, University of California Press, Los Angeles, 1951.

Sartre, Jean-Paul, *Nausea*, translated by Lloyd Alexander, A New Directions Paperback, Norfolk, Connecticut, 1938.

———, *No Exit* and *The Flies*, translated by Stuart Gilbert, Alfred A. Knopf, New York, 1948.

———, *Existentialism and Human Emotions*, The Wisdom Library, a division of Philosophical Library, New York, 1957.

———, *Being and Nothingness*, translated by Hazel E. Barnes, Philosophical Library, New York, 1956.

———, *The Emotions: Outline of a Theory*, translated by B. Frechtman, The Wisdom Library, a division of Philosophical Library, New York, 1948.

———, *Essays in Aesthetics*, translated by Wade Baskin, The Citadel Press, New York, 1963.

———, *The Psychology of Imagination*, The Citadel Press, New York, 1948.

———, *Literature and Existentialism,* translated by B. Frechtman, The Citadel Press, New York, 1949.

———, *The Transcendence of the Ego*, translated by Forrest Williams and Robert Kirkpatrick, the Noonday Press, 1937.

———, *Literary and Philosophical Essays*, translated by Annette Michelson, Collier Books, New York, 1955.

Scheffler, Israel, ed., *Philosophy and Education,* Allyn and Bacon, Inc., Boston, 1958.

———, *The Language of Education*, Charles C. Thomas, Springfield, Illinois, 1960.

Schilpp, P. A., ed., *The Philosophy of John Dewey*, Tudor Publishing Company, New York, 1939.

Werkmeister, W. H., *The Basis and Structure of Knowledge*, Harper and Brothers, New York, 1948.

Wisdom, John, *Philosophy and Pschyo-Analysis*, Basil Blackwell, Oxford, 1957.

Wittgenstein, Ludwig, *The Blue and Brown Books*, Harper Torchbooks, The Academy Library, Harper and Row, New York, 1958.

———, *Philosophical Investigations*, translated by G. E. M. Anscombe, The Macmillan Company, New York, 1953.